Kika Wa

G000153733

Adoption N

Law, regulations, guidance and standards

Fergus Smith and Roy Stewart
with Deborah Cullen

British Association for Adoption & Fostering
(BAAF)
Saffron House
6–10 Kirby Street
London EC1N 8TS
www.baaf.org.uk

Charity registration 275689

Reprinted 2009

British Library Cataloguing in Publication Data
A catalogue record for this book is available
from the British Library

ISBN 1 903699 87 8

Designed by Andrew Haig & Associates
Typeset by Avon DataSet Ltd, Bidford on Avon
Printed in Great Britain by The Lavenham Press

BAAF is the leading UK-wide membership
organisation for all those concerned with
adoption, fostering and child care issues.

Contents

*All references in brackets are to the Adoption and Children Act 2002
(ACA 2002) unless otherwise stated.
CA 1989 = Children Act 1989*

Notes about the authors

Fergus Smith is the Director of Children Act Enterprises Ltd (www.caeuk.org), an independent social work consultancy which undertakes research, consultancy, training and independent investigation. Fergus is also the author of over a dozen pocket-sized guides to family and criminal law written in consultation with acknowledged experts in their field.

Roy Stewart is an independent child care consultant and trainer, an independent chair of adoption and fostering panels, and Associate Consultant with Children Act Enterprises. Roy has extensive experience as a practitioner and manager in local authority adoption and fostering services.

Deborah Cullen is the Legal Group Co-ordinator at BAAF. She writes Legal Notes for *Adoption & Fostering*, BAAF's quarterly journal, and has authored several articles and books on childcare law. Deborah was a consultant to the authors.

Part I

Principles, concepts and statutory provisions

Introduction

- This guide is for use by those in England and (unless otherwise specified) Wales, whose work with children and their families does, or might, involve adoption.

- It is intended to provide easy access to and reinforce understanding of the Adoption and Children Act 2002 (fully implemented on 30.12.05) as well as associated regulations, guidance, rules and national minimum standards.

  Regulations that apply exclusively to Wales are not included in this guide.

- **Part I** of the book summarises the principles and concepts underpinning, as well as the main provisions of, the new law.

- It is laid out in the following order which reflects the anticipated needs of practitioners and includes, where required, a brief reference to the relevant regulation or court rule:

  - **principles and concepts**

  - **adoption service**

  - **authority to place**

  - **consequences of placement**

  - **removal of children**

  - **adoption orders**

  - **disclosure of information**

  - **status of adopted children**

  - **the registers**

  - **adoptions with a foreign element**

  - **miscellaneous provisions**

- **special guardianship**

- **advertisements and the Adoption and Children Act register**

■ **Part II** offers a comprehensive summary of relevant regulations.

■ **Part III** provides a summary of the National Minimum Standards for adoption agencies and adoption support agencies.

■ **Part IV** contains a brief summary of some of the key rules governing court procedures under the Act.

■ A subject index enables rapid access to specific subjects.

This guide should be used only to supplement, not replace, reference to source material and competent legal advice.

Principles and concepts

■ The Adoption and Children Act 2002 (ACA) is founded upon the following overarching principles:

- **paramountcy of the child's welfare** – in all decisions by courts and adoption agencies, including whether to dispense with a parent's consent to adoption;

- **a "welfare checklist"** comparable to its Children Act 1989 equivalent but reflecting adoption-related issues;

- **avoidance of undue delay** in planning for permanence and adoption when children cannot be cared for by their birth family;

- **no order** – unless the court considers that making the order would be better for the child than not doing so.

■ The Act is also conceptually underpinned by its:

- enhancement of permanence options through extension (when appropriate) of residence orders to 18 years and by introducing "special guardianship";

- introduction of the possibility of unmarried couples adopting jointly;

- encouragement of people to adopt by obliging local authorities to ensure that support and required financial assistance are available to those affected by adoption;

- acknowledgement of the life-long impact of adoption on all parties; and

- establishment of a more consistent approach to the release of sensitive and identifying information contained in adoption records.

Exercise of powers by court or adoption agency [s.1]

- Section 1 applies whenever a court or adoption agency is coming to a decision relating to the adoption of a child [s.1(1)].

- The paramount consideration of the court or adoption agency must be the child's welfare, throughout her/his life [s.1(2)].

- The court or adoption agency must at all times bear in mind that, in general, any delay in coming to the decision is likely to prejudice the child's welfare [s.1(3)].

- The court or adoption agency must have regard to the following matters (among others):

  - the child's ascertainable wishes and feelings regarding the decision (considered in the light of her/his age and understanding);

  - the child's particular needs;

  - the likely effect on the child (throughout life) of having ceased to be a member of the original family and becoming an adopted person;

  - the child's age, sex, background and any of the child's characteristics which the court or agency considers relevant;

- any harm (within the meaning of section 31(9) Children Act 1989 as amended) which the child has suffered or is at risk of suffering;

- the relationship which the child has with relatives, and with any other person in relation to whom the court or agency considers it relevant, including the likelihood of any such relationship continuing and the value to the child of its doing so; secondly, the ability and willingness of any of the child's relatives, or of any such person, to provide the child with a secure environment in which the child can develop, and otherwise to meet the child's needs; and thirdly, the wishes and feelings of any of the child's relatives, or of any such person, regarding the child [s.1(4)].

■ In placing the child for adoption, the adoption agency must give due consideration to her/his religious persuasion, racial origin and cultural and linguistic background [s.1(5)].

■ The court or adoption agency must always consider the whole range of powers available to it in the child's case (whether under this Act or the Children Act 1989) and must not make any order under this Act unless it considers that making the order would be better for the child than not doing so [s.1(6)].

■ In section 7, 'coming to a decision relating to the adoption of a child', in relation to a court, includes:

- in any proceedings where the orders that might be made include the making or revoking of an adoption or placement order or making, varying or revoking a section 26 contact order;

- making a decision about granting leave in respect of any action (other than initiation of proceedings in any court) which may be taken by an adoption agency or individual under this Act.

■ It does **not** include coming to a decision about granting leave in any other circumstances [s.1(7)].

For the purposes of section 1, references to relationships are not confined to legal relationships and references to a relative, in relation to a child, include the child's mother and father [s.1(8)].

The adoption service

Basic definitions [s.2]

■ The services maintained by local authorities under section 3(1) described below may be collectively referred to as 'the adoption service', and a local authority or registered adoption society may be referred to as an "adoption agency" [s.2(1)].

■ A 'registered adoption society' means a voluntary organisation which is an adoption society registered under Part 2 of the Care Standards Act 2000.

■ In relation to the provision of any facility of the adoption service, references to a registered adoption society or an adoption agency do not include an adoption society which is not registered in respect of that facility [s.2(2)] i.e. under section 13(3) Care Standards Act 2000 the registration authority may attach a condition to registration including a condition that the body is not registered in respect of a particular facility.

■ A registered adoption society is to be treated as registered in respect of any facility of the adoption service unless it is a condition of its registration that it does not provide that facility [s.2(3)].

■ Adoption societies applying under Part 2 of the Care Standards Act 2000 must be incorporated bodies [s.2(4)].

■ In the ACA 2002:

  • 'the 1989 Act' means the Children Act 1989;

  • 'adoption society' means a body whose functions consist of or include making arrangements for the adoption of children;

- 'voluntary organisation' means a body other than a public or local authority, the activities of which are not carried on for profit [s.2(5)];

- 'adoption support services' means counselling, advice and information, and any other services prescribed in the Adoption Support Services Regulations 2005 [s.2(6)].

■ The power to make regulations, as referred to above, is to be exercised so as to secure that local authorities provide financial support [s.2(7)].

■ In sections 2–17 ACA 2002, references to adoption are to the adoption of persons, wherever they may be habitually resident, effected under the law of any country or territory, within or outside the British Islands [s.2(8)].

Maintenance of adoption service [s.3]

■ Each local authority must continue to maintain within its area (and for that purpose must provide the requisite facilities for) a service designed to meet the needs, in relation to adoption, of:

- children who may be adopted, their parents and guardians;

- persons wishing to adopt a child; and

- adopted persons, their adoptive parents, birth parents and former guardians [s.3(1)].

■ Those facilities must include making, and participating in, arrangements for the:

- adoption of children, and

- provision of adoption support services [s.3(2)].

■ As part of the service, the arrangements made for the purposes of adoption support services:

- must extend to the provision of adoption support services to those described in the Adoption Support Services Regulations 2005, and

- may extend to the provision of those services to others [s.3(3)].

■ A local authority may provide any of the requisite facilities by securing its provision by:

- registered adoption societies, or

- others identified in regulation 5 of the Adoption Support Services Regulations 2005 of persons who may provide the facilities in question [s.3(4)].

■ The facilities must be provided in conjunction with the local authority's other social services and with registered adoption societies in its area, so that help may be given in a co-ordinated manner without duplication, omission or avoidable delay [s.3(5)].

■ The social services referred to in section 3(5) are the functions of a local authority which are social services functions within the meaning of the Local Authority Social Services Act 1970 [s.3(6)].

Assessments etc. for adoption support services [s.4]
■ A local authority must carry out an assessment of that person's needs for adoption support services at the request of any:

- of the persons mentioned in section 3(1), or

- other person identified in regulation 13 of the Adoption Support Services Regulations 2005 [s.4(1)].

■ A local authority may, at the request of any person, carry out an assessment of that person's needs for adoption support services [s.4(2)].

■ A local authority may request the help of registered adoption societies or of persons identified in regulation 14 of the Adoption Support Services

Regulations 2005 in carrying out an assessment [s.4(3)].

- Where, as a result of an assessment, a local authority decides that a person has needs for adoption support services, it must then decide whether to provide any such services to that person [s.4(4)].

- If the local authority decides to provide any adoption support services to a person, and the circumstances are as described in regulation 16 of the Adoption Support Services Regulations 2005:

  - it must prepare a plan for their provision and keep the plan under review [s.4(5)].

- Regulations made under section 4(6) make provision about assessments, preparing and reviewing plans, the provision of adoption support services in accordance with plans and reviewing the provision of adoption support services.

- A local authority may carry out an assessment of the needs of any person under section 4 at the same time as an assessment of her/his needs is made under any other enactment [s.4(8)].

- The local authority must notify the relevant health or education authority if at any time during the assessment of the needs of any person under section 4, it appears that there may be a need for the provision to that person of services from such authorities [s.4(9)].

- Where it appears to a local authority that another local authority could, by taking any specified action, help in the exercise of any of its functions under section 4, it may request the help of that other authority, specifying the action in question [s.4(10)].

- A local authority whose help is so requested must comply with the request if it is consistent with the exercise of its functions [s.4(11)].

Local authority plans for adoption services [s.5]

■ Section 64 Children Act 2004 repealed the obligation introduced by section 5 ACA 2002 for production of local authority plans for adoption services and replaced it with an obligation under section 17 of that Act to produce regular 'children and young people's plans'.

De-registered, inactive or defunct adoption societies [ss.6&7]

■ There is a power for the appropriate Minister to direct such a society or, if necessary, the local authority to take appropriate action for the transfer of the functions of such a society.

Adoption support agencies [s.8]

■ In the ACA 2002, 'adoption support agency' means an 'undertaking', the purpose of which, or one of the purposes of which, is the provision of adoption support services. However, an undertaking is not an adoption support agency:

- merely because it provides information in connection with adoption other than for the purpose mentioned in section 98(1), or

- if it is excepted by virtue of section 8(2) summarised below [s.8(1)].

■ The following are for the purposes of section 8(1) 'excepted':

- a registered adoption society, whether or not registered in respect of provision of adoption support services;

- a local authority;

- a local education authority (within the meaning of the Education Act 1996);

- a Special Health Authority, Primary Care Trust (in Wales, a Health Authority or Local Health Board) or NHS trust;

- the Registrar General;

- any person, or description of persons, excepted in regulation 4 of the Adoption Support Agencies (England) and Adoption Agencies (Miscellaneous Amendments) Regulations 2005 [s.8(2)].

Section 4 Care Standards Act 2000 (basic definitions) is amended by section 8(3) ACA 2002 to provide recognition of adoption support agencies and to ensure both Acts are compatible. The purpose of these provisions is to allow (properly regulated) agencies other than adoption agencies to provide support services e.g. specialist birth records counselling and other services set out in the national framework.

REGULATIONS

■ Sections 9 and 10 contain regulation-making powers in respect of the adoption functions of local authorities, voluntary adoption agencies and adoption support agencies. Section 11 allows regulations to prescribe fees for certain services including intercountry adoption.

Independent review of determinations [s.12]

■ Regulations under section 9 (the Independent Review of Determinations (Adoption) Regulations 2005) establish a procedure under which any person in respect of whom a qualifying determination has been made by an adoption agency may apply to a panel constituted by the appropriate Minister for a review of that determination [s.12(1)].

■ The appropriate Minister may make an arrangement with an organisation under which panel functions are performed by the organisation on her/his behalf [s.12(4)].

■ If the appropriate Minister makes such an arrangement (which may include payment to the organisation by the Minister) the organisation is to perform its functions in accordance with any general or special directions given by the appropriate Minister [s.12(5); (6)].

■ The Welsh Assembly is able to ask the English Secretary of State to provide its required independent review mechanism [s.12(7)].

In section 12, 'organisation' includes a public body and a private or voluntary organisation [s.12(8)].

SUPPLEMENTAL
Information concerning adoption [ss.13–15]
- Adoption agencies and courts are obliged to comply with directions from the appropriate Minister to provide statistical and other information relating to adoption [s.13].

- Section 14 allows the appropriate Minister to exercise powers when a local authority has failed to comply with its duties under the Act or the Adoption (Intercountry Aspects) Act 1999.

- Section 15 contains powers enabling the Minister to inspect premises or records.

Distribution of functions in relation to registered adoption societies [s.16]
- Section 16 ACA 2002 inserts a new section 36A into Part 2 Care Standards Act 2000 which makes provision for the distribution (across England and Wales) of functions in relation to registered adoption societies.

- Paragraph 106 of Schedule 3 dis-applies the requirement for separate branch registration in relation to registered adoption societies which will not therefore need to be separately registered.

- Section 17(5) provides that the functions in relation to inspection are exercisable where the premises are in England, by CSCI (Commission for Social Care Inspection) and in Wales by the Assembly, which will enable CSCI to inspect branches of agencies operating in England but registered in Wales and vice versa.

Inquiries [s.17]

- Section 3 Children Act 2004 introduced the role of the Children's Commissioner in England and she/he is empowered to conduct inquiries into matters connected with the functions of an adoption agency if she/he considers that an individual case raises matters of public policy relevant to other children.

- Such inquiries may be partly or wholly conducted in private.

Authority to place

- The following sections summarise the new framework for placements and its:

  - requirement that agencies must be 'authorised' to place a child, and

  - establishment of two available routes for agency placement, i.e. placement with consent and placement by means of placement order.

  See Adoption Guidance Annex A paragraphs 9–62 for detailed advice on the new placement framework.

  Placement for adoption by adoption agency [s.18]
- An adoption agency may:

  - place a child for adoption with prospective adopters; or

  - where it has placed a child with any persons, leave the child with them as prospective adopters [s.18(1)]; and

  - except in the case of a child who is less than six weeks old, may only do so under section 19 or a placement order [s.18(1)].

- An adoption agency may **only** place a child for adoption with prospective adopters if the agency is satisfied that the child ought to be placed for adoption [s.18(2)].

- A child who is placed or authorised to be placed for adoption with prospective adopters by a local authority is looked after by the authority [s.18(3)].

- If an application for an adoption order (including a Scottish or Northern Irish order) has been made by any persons in respect of a child and has not been disposed of:

  - an adoption agency, which placed the child with those persons, may leave the child with them until the application is disposed of; but

  - apart from that, the child may not be placed for adoption with any prospective adopters [s.18(4)].

- 'Placing a child for adoption' includes where an agency has placed a child with any persons, and leaves the child with them as prospective adopters [s.18(5)].

- An agency is 'authorised to place a child for adoption' where consent has been given under section 19 or the court has made a placement order [s.18(6)].

  Section 18 is subject to sections 30–35 (removal of children placed by adoption agencies).

  Placing children with parental consent [s.19]
- The agency is authorised to place the child for adoption where an adoption agency is satisfied that each parent or guardian of a child has **consented** (and has not withdrawn the consent) to the child being placed for adoption with:

  - prospective adopters identified in the consent, or

  - any prospective adopters chosen by the agency [s.19(1)].

- Consent to a child's placement with identified adopters may also include consent to a subsequent placement with **any** prospective adopters chosen by the agency if the first placement ends [s.19(2)].

- Section 19(1) does not apply where:

  - an application has been made on which a care order might be made and the application has not been disposed of; or

  - a care order or placement order has been made after the consent was given [s.19(3)].

- References to a child placed for adoption under section 19 include a child who was placed under section 19 with prospective adopters and continues to be placed with them, whether or not consent to the placement has been withdrawn [s.19(4)].

  This section is subject to section 52 (parental etc. consent) [s.19(5)].

  ### Advance consent to adoption [s.20]

- A parent or guardian of a child who consents to the child being placed for adoption by an adoption agency under section 19 may, at the same or any subsequent time, consent to the making of a future adoption order [s.20(1)].

- Consent under section 20:

  - where the parent or guardian has consented to the child being placed for adoption with prospective adopters identified in the consent, may be consent to adoption by them; or

  - may be consent to adoption by any prospective adopters to be chosen by the agency [s.20(2)].

- A person may withdraw any consent given under section 20 [s.20(3)].

- A person who gives consent under section 20 may, at the same or any subsequent time, by notice given to the adoption agency:

- state that she/he does not wish to be informed of any application for an adoption order; or

- withdraw such a statement [s.20(4)].

'Notice' means written notice.

Witnessing consent [reg.20 the Adoption Agencies Regulations 2005]

■ Regulation 20 requires agencies to request the appointment of a CAFCASS officer or a Welsh Family Proceedings Officer to witness consent to placement or future adoption under section 19 or section 20 of the Act, and to send the information specified in Schedule 2.

■ Where the person giving consent is outside England or Wales, regulation 20A deals with the procedure for witnessing consent.

Placement orders [s.21]

■ A placement order is an order made by the court authorising a local authority to place a child for adoption with any prospective adopters who may be chosen by the authority [s.21(1)].

■ The court may not make a placement order in respect of a child **unless** the child is subject to a care order, the court is satisfied the conditions in section 31(2) Children Act 1989 (conditions for making a care order) are met or the child has no parent or guardian [s.21(2)] **and** the court is satisfied that:

- each parent or guardian has consented to the child being placed for adoption with any prospective adopters who may be chosen by the local authority and has not withdrawn the consent, or that

- the parent's or guardian's consent should be dispensed with [s.21(3)].

Section 21(3) is subject to section 52 (parental etc. consent).

- A placement order continues in force until:

  - it is revoked under section 24;

  - an adoption order is made in respect of the child; or

  - the child marries, enters into a civil partnership or attains the age of 18 years [s.21(4)].

Applications for placement orders [s.22]

- A local authority **must** apply to the court for a placement order in respect of a child if:

  - the child is placed for adoption by it, or is being provided with accommodation by it;

  - no adoption agency is authorised to place the child for adoption;

  - the child has no parent or guardian or the authority considers that the conditions in section 31(2) Children Act 1989 are met; **and**

  - the authority is satisfied that the child ought to be placed for adoption [s.22(1)].

- The appropriate local authority must apply to the court for a placement order if it is satisfied that the child ought to be placed for adoption, and:

  - an application has been made (and has not been disposed of) on which a care order might be made in respect of a child; or

  - a child is subject to a care order and the appropriate local authority is not authorised to place the child for adoption [s.22(2)].

- The authority **may** apply to the court for a placement order if:

  - a child is subject to a care order; and

- the appropriate local authority is authorised to place the child for adoption under section 19 [s.22(3)].

■ Section 22(1)–(3) does not apply in respect of a child, if:

- any persons have given notice of intention to adopt, unless the period of four months beginning with the giving of the notice has expired without them applying for an adoption order or their application for such an order has been withdrawn or refused; or

- an application for an adoption order has been made and has not been disposed of [s.22(5)].

■ The court may give any directions it considers appropriate for medical or psychiatric examination or other assessment of the child (but a child who is of sufficient understanding to make an informed decision may refuse to submit to the examination or other assessment) where:

- an application for a placement order in respect of a child has been made and not been disposed of, and

- no interim care order is in force [s.22(6)].

■ The appropriate local authority:

- in relation to a care order, is the local authority in whose care the child is placed by the order; and

- in relation to an application on which a care order might be made, is the local authority which makes the application [s.22(7)].

Varying placement orders [s.23]

■ The court may vary a placement order so as to substitute another local authority for the local authority authorised by the order to place the child for adoption [s.23(1)].

■ The variation may only be made on the joint application of both authorities [s.23(2)].

Revoking placement orders [s.24]

■ The court may revoke a placement order on the application of any person [s.24(1)].

■ But, someone other than the child or the local authority may apply, only if:

• the court has given leave to apply, and

• the child is not placed for adoption by the authority [s.24(2)].

■ The court cannot give leave unless satisfied that there has been a change in circumstances since the order was made [s.24(3)].

■ If the court determines, on an application for an adoption order, not to make the order, it may revoke any placement order in respect of the child [s.24(4)].

■ The child may not, without the court's leave, be placed for adoption under the order, where:

• an application for revocation of a placement order has been made and has not been disposed of; and

• the child is not placed for adoption by the authority [s.24(5)].

Consequences of placement

■ Consent to placement or the making of a placement order has consequences for:

• parental responsibility;

- contact; and

- surname and (more than temporary) removal from the UK.

■ These consequences are spelt out immediately below and summarised in tabular form at the end of this section.

Parental responsibility [s.25]

■ If a child is placed for adoption under section 19, an adoption agency is authorised to place a child for adoption under that section, or a placement order is in force in respect of a child, parental responsibility for the child is given to the agency concerned [s.25(1); (2)].

■ While the child is placed with prospective adopters, parental responsibility is also given to them [s.25(3)].

The agency may determine that the parental responsibility of any parent or guardian, or of prospective adopters, should be restricted to the extent it decides is necessary [s.25(4)].

Contact [s.26]

■ On an adoption agency being authorised to place a child for adoption, or upon placing a child for adoption who is less than six weeks old, any provision for contact under the Children Act 1989 Act ceases to have effect [s.26(1)].

■ While an adoption agency is so authorised, or a child is placed for adoption:

- no application may be made for any contact order under the Children Act 1989; but

- the court may make an order under section 26 requiring the person with whom the child lives, or is to live, to allow her/him to visit or stay with the person named in the order, or for the person named in the order and the child to have contact with each other [s.26(2)].

- An application for an order under section 26 may be made by:

  - the child or agency;

  - any parent, guardian or relative;

  - any person in whose favour there was provision for contact under the Children Act 1989 which ceased to have effect by virtue of section 26(1);

  - if a residence order was in force immediately before the adoption agency was authorised to place the child for adoption (or placed the child for adoption at a time when she/he was less than six weeks old), the person in whose favour the order was made;

  - another individual if she/he had care of the child immediately before that time by virtue of an order made in the exercise of the High Court's inherent jurisdiction with respect to children;

  - any person who has obtained the court's leave to make the application [s.26(3)].

- When making a placement order, the court may on its own initiative make an order under section 26.

- Section 26 does not prevent an application for a contact order under section 8 Children Act 1989 being made where the application is to be heard together with an application for an adoption order in respect of the child.

  In section 26, 'provision for contact under the 1989 Act' means a contact order under section 8 or an order under section 34 of that Act (parental contact with children in care) [s.26(6)].

Contact: supplementary [s.27]

- An order under section 26:

  - has effect while the adoption agency is authorised to place the child for adoption or the child is placed for adoption, but

  - may be varied or revoked by the court on an application by the child, the agency or a person named in the order [s.27(1)].

- The agency may refuse to allow contact that would otherwise be required by a section 26 order if:

  - it is satisfied that it is necessary to do so in order to safeguard or promote the child's welfare, and

  - refusal is decided upon as a matter of urgency and does not last for more than seven days [s.27(2)].

- Regulation 47 of the Adoption Agencies Regulations 2005 specifies the:

  - steps to be taken by an agency which has exercised its power under section 27(2);

  - circumstances in which, and conditions subject to which, terms of any order under section 26 may be departed from by agreement between the agency and any person for whose contact with the child the order provides;

  - notification by an agency of any variation or suspension of arrangements made (other than under an order under section 26) with a view to allowing any person contact with the child [s.27(3)].

- Before making a placement order, the court must:

  - consider the arrangements which the adoption agency has made, or proposes to make, for allowing any person contact with the child, and

  - invite the parties to the proceedings to comment [s.27(4)].

■ An order under section 26 may provide for contact on any conditions the court considers appropriate [s.27(5)].

Further consequences of placement [s.28]

■ Where a child has been placed with parental consent or an adoption agency is authorised to place a child for adoption under section 19:

- a parent or guardian of the child may not apply for a residence order unless an application for an adoption order has been made and she/he has obtained the court's leave under section 47(3) or (5);

- if an application has been made for an adoption order, a guardian of the child may not apply for a special guardianship order unless she/he has obtained the court's leave under section 47(3) or (5) [s.28(1)].

■ Where a child is placed for adoption or an adoption agency is authorised to place a child for adoption under section 19, or a placement order is in force in respect of her/him, then (whether or not she/he is in England and Wales) a person may not, unless the court gives leave, or each parent or guardian of the child gives written consent [s.28(2)]:

- cause the child to be known by a new surname, or

- remove the child from the UK [s.28(2);(3)].

Section 28(3) does not prevent the removal of a child from the UK for a period of less than one month by a person who provides the child's home.

Further consequences of placement orders [s.29]

■ Where a placement order is made in respect of a child and either the child is subject to a care order, or the court at the same time makes a care order in respect of the child, the care order does not have effect at any time when the placement order is in force [s.29(1)].

■ On the making of a placement order in respect of a child, any order mentioned in section 8(1) Children Act 1989 and any supervision order in respect of the child, ceases to have effect [s.29(2)].

■ Where a placement order is in force, the following orders may **not** be made in respect of the child:

• prohibited steps order, residence order or specific issue order, and

• supervision or child assessment order [s.29(3)].

■ The first of the above two prohibitions does not apply in respect of a residence order if:

• an application for an adoption order has been made in respect of the child, and

• the residence order is applied for by a parent or guardian who has obtained the court's leave under section 47(3) or (5) or by any other person who has obtained the court's leave under this subsection [s.29(4)].

■ Where a placement order is in force, no special guardianship order may be made in respect of the child unless:

• an application has been made for an adoption order, and

• the person applying for the special guardianship order has obtained the court's leave under section 29(5) or, if she/he is a guardian of the child, has obtained the court's leave under section 47(5) [s.29(5)].

■ A person who has 'leave to apply' is not required to give three months' notice of her/his application for a special guardianship order [s.14A(7) Children Act 1989].

■ An application for a special guardianship order can only be made at the final hearing and with leave of the court [s.14C(1)(b) Children Act 1989].

Summary of placement routes and their consequences

ROUTE TO PLACEMENT	**CONSEQUENCES**
Consent [s.19]	Agency is given parental responsibility and can restrict parents' exercise of her/his responsibility.
	Any Children Act 1989 provisions for contact are replaced to be dealt with under sections 26 and 27.
	In case of a local authority, child is looked after though some 'looked after children' regulations will not apply.
	Without written consent of each parent/guardian or the court's permission, nobody may change child's name or remove her/him from UK (for a month or more).
	A parent or guardian may withdraw consent up to lodging of adoption order application.
	Once placed, prospective adopters have parental responsibility (may be restricted by the agency) and a parent or guardian may not apply for a residence order (except with court's permission, within adoption application).
	A parent is not permitted to oppose the grant of an adoption order unless the court grants permission (and it can do so only if satisfied there has been a change of circumstances).
	In addition to the above consequences:
Placement Order [s.21]	Any care order in force is suspended for the duration of the placement order.

Any Children Act 1989 section 8 or supervision order eases to have effect.

No Children Act 1989 section 8, supervision, child assessment or special guardianship order may be applied for (except, within the adoption application, the court may give permission for making an application for a residence or special guardianship order).

Placement order ceases when child is adopted, reaches 18 or is married or enters civil partnership.

A placement order can be revoked on an application to court but only local authority or court may apply without leave – others can apply only with the court's permission (which cannot be given if the child has been placed for adoption) and only if the court is satisfied there has been a change of circumstances.

Removal of children who are or may be placed by adoption agencies

- The ACA 2002 introduces measures to ensure children placed for adoption are not precipitately removed.

- The measures distinguish between agency and non-agency cases.

- Key points are that:

  - the agency acts as a "go-between" and if the child is placed with prospective adopters, only the agency may remove her/him;

  - even where the parent has a right to the return of the child, 7 or 14 days are allowed (according to circumstances) for negotiation and preparation of the child;

- there are criminal sanctions for removing a child contrary to, or failing to return a child to the agency in accordance with the law (and recovery orders may be made against those who fail to comply);

- the making of an application for a placement order has the effect of barring a child's removal from local authority accommodation;

- where the child is subject to a care order, the Children Act 1989 provisions apply in place of sections 31–33 of this Act;

- these provisions do not prevent the removal of a child who is arrested nor the exercise of local authority or other powers apart from the right of a parent to remove her/his child from local authority accommodation under section 20 Children Act 1989 i.e. an emergency protection order or use of police powers of protection remains possible.

Recovery by parents etc where child not placed or is a baby [s.31]

- Section 31(2) applies where:

  - the child is not yet placed for adoption but section 19 consent was given (even if subsequently withdrawn);

  - a baby under six weeks old was placed and remains with prospective adopters (without consent under section 19) even if she/he is now more than six weeks old.

- In these circumstances, if the parent informs the agency that she/he wishes the child to be returned to her/him, the agency must return the child within seven days, unless it applies or has applied for a placement order.

- Where the child is actually placed, the agency must give notice to the prospective adopters who must return the child to the agency within seven days. The agency must then immediately return the child to the parent.

- If the prospective adopters fail to comply, the parent is not permitted in consequence of section 30(1) to remove her/his child. In such circumstances, the agency or parent may apply for a section 41 recovery order (see below).

It is the application for a placement order that effectively freezes a parent's right to have her/his child returned.

Recovery by parents etc where child not placed and consent withdrawn [s.32]

■ Section 32 applies where a child is placed for adoption by an adoption agency following consent to placement under section 19 and where that consent has been withdrawn.

Withdrawal of consent after an application for adoption has been issued is ineffective.

■ **Unless** an application is, or has been made, for a placement order, the agency must give the prospective adopters notice and they must return the child to the agency within 14 days and the agency must then immediately return the child to her/his parent.

■ **If before notice is given** to the prospective adopters, an application for an adoption order, special guardianship order or residence order (or for leave to apply for a special guardianship order or residence order) has been made in respect of the child, the prospective adopters will not be required to return the child unless the court so orders.

■ Regulation 38 of the Adoption Agencies Regulations 2005 indicates that, when consent is withdrawn, a local authority must immediately review its decision to place a child for adoption and consider whether to apply for a placement order.

■ In the case of a voluntary agency, it must immediately inform the local authority where the child is living.

Birth parents need to be advised that if they were to withdraw consent to

*placement but did not inform the agency that they wanted the child
returned, the prospective adopters might issue an adoption (or other)
application before any notice was served on them. It would then be for the
court to decide whether to order the child's return.*

Recovery by parents etc where child placed and placement order refused [s.33]

- Section 33 applies where a child was placed for adoption by a local authority under section 19 and the local authority is unsuccessful in an application for a placement order.

- Where the parent requests the return of the child, the court will fix a date for the prospective adopters to return the child to the local authority at which time it must return the child to her/his parents.

Placement orders: prohibition on removal [s.34]

- Section 34 prohibits the removal of a child while a placement order is in force and also restricts the ability of a parent or anyone else to remove the child when the placement order is revoked.

- The return of the child to the parent is a matter to be determined by the court.

- If the child is actually placed with prospective adopters at the time of revocation (likely to be rare since only the local authority or the child can apply for revocation if the child is placed), the court will determine whether/when the child is to be returned by the former prospective adopters to the local authority.

Return of child in other cases [s.35]

- This section deals with placement disruptions that are independent of any action or notice by birth parents.

- Prospective adopters may give the agency notice of their wish to return the child and the agency may give notice to the prospective adopters that, in its opinion, the child should not remain with them.

- In either case:

  - the child is to be returned to and received by the agency within seven days of the notice; and

  - the agency must inform the parent/guardian.

  The latter requirement is significant, especially when a placement order exists since the parent can only apply for revocation of a placement order if the child is not placed for adoption.

- Regulation 36 of the Adoption Agencies Regulations 2005 requires the local authority to review (28 to 42 days following the disruption) the case of a child returned by prospective adopters.

Removal of children in non-agency cases

Restrictions on removal [s.36]

- This section places restrictions on the removal of a child from prospective adopters who have:

  - applied for an adoption order (while the application is pending);

  - given notice of intention to adopt; or

  - applied for leave to apply for an adoption order under section 42(6).

- In general, the court's leave will be required to remove the child except where the person concerned is acting under statutory powers (other than a parent's right under section 20 Children Act 1989 to remove her/his child from local authority accommodation).

- There are two exceptions:

- foster carer cases and

- step-parent cases.

■ If local authority **foster carers** give notice of their intention to adopt a child whom they have been looking after for more than one year but less than five years, the person with parental responsibility may exercise the power to remove the child under section 20(8) Children Act 1989 without the court's leave.

■ In the case of **step-parents**, where the partner of a parent has given notice of intention to adopt a child who has had her/his home with that partner for less than three out of the last five years, a parent or guardian may remove the child without the court's leave.

The above right would not presumably override the restrictions that might apply if the other parent had a residence order in her/his favour.

Applicants for adoption [s.37]

■ At any time when a child is living with anyone with whom she/he is not placed by an adoption agency, but those people have applied for an adoption order and the application is pending, the following may remove the child:

- a person who has the court's leave, or

- a local authority or other person in the exercise of a power conferred by any law (except section 20(8) Children Act 1989 – removal of a child from accommodation [s.37(1)].

Local authority foster carers [s.38]

■ Section 38 applies if the child is living with local authority foster carers.

■ If the child has lived with the foster carers at all times in five years before her/his removal and the foster carers have given notice of intention to adopt, or an application has been made for leave under section 42(6) and is still pending, the following may remove the child:

- a person who has the court's leave, or
- a local authority or other person in the exercise of a power conferred by any law – other than section 20(8) Children Act 1989 [s.38(2) & (3)].

- If the child has lived with the foster carers at all times in the one year before removal, and the foster carers have given notice of intention to adopt, the following may remove the child:

  - a person with parental responsibility for the child who is exercising the power in section 20(8) Children Act 1989;
  - a person who has the court's leave; or
  - a local authority or other person in the exercise of a power conferred by any law, other than section 20(8) Children Act 1989 [s.38(5)].

Partners of parents [s.39]

- Section 39 applies if a child lives with a partner of a parent and that partner has given notice of intention to adopt [s.39(1)].

- If the child has lived with the partner for not less than three years (continuous or not) during the five years before removal, the following may remove the child:

  - a person who has the court's leave, or
  - a local authority or other person in the exercise of a power conferred by any law, other than section 20(8) Children Act 1989 [s.39(2)].

- In other cases where the partner has given notice of intention to adopt, the child may be removed by a:

  - parent or guardian;

- person who has the court's leave; or

- local authority or other person in the exercise of a power conferred by any enactment, other than section 20(8) Children Act 1989 [s.39(3)].

Other non-agency cases [s.40]

- In other non-agency cases, so long as the persons concerned have given notice of intention to adopt, or applied for leave and the application is pending, the following may remove the child:

  - a person who has the court's leave, or

  - a local authority or other person in the exercise of a power conferred by any law (other than section 20(8) Children Act 1989).

BREACH OF RESTRICTIONS ON REMOVAL
Recovery orders [s.41]

- Where it appears to the court that a child has been unlawfully removed or there are reasonable grounds for believing that a person intends to unlawfully remove a child, or has failed to comply with requirements related to removal or return, the court may, on the application of any person, by an order:

  - direct any person who can to produce the child on request to a specified person;

  - authorise removal of the child by a specified person;

  - require any person who has information about the child's whereabouts to disclose it on request to a police or court officer;

  - authorise police to enter any premises specified in the order and search for the child, using reasonable force if necessary.

- The persons who may be specified are:

  - a person named by the court;

- the police; or

- a person authorised by the adoption agency that is authorised to place the child for adoption.

■ A person who intentionally obstructs a person exercising such a power of removal conferred by the order is guilty of an offence.

Adoption orders

■ The following section outlines some 'pre-conditions' for making adoption orders:

- child to live with adopter;

- agency or local authority court report on suitability of applicant/s;

- a notice of intention to adopt; and

- the suitability of adopters.

■ The section also defines and includes conditions for the making of an adoption order which are related to:

- parental consent;

- child's placement for adoption with the prospective adopters;

- child's status as 'freed for adoption' (under Scottish/Northern Irish law);

- the age and marital status of child;

- any previous application;

- the age and parental status of the applicant/s.

PRELIMINARIES TO ADOPTION
Child to live with adopters before application made [s.42]

- An application for an adoption order may not be made unless specified conditions (that vary according to the child's circumstances) are met.

- If the child was placed for adoption with the applicant/s by an adoption agency or in pursuance of an order of the High Court, or the applicant is a parent of the child:

  - the condition is she/he must have lived with one or other or both applicant/s at all times during the 10 weeks preceding the application [s.42(2)].

- If the applicant or one of the applicants is the partner of a parent of the child, the condition is that the child must have lived with the applicant/s at all times during the period of six months preceding the application [s.42(3)].

- If the applicants are local authority foster carers, the condition is that the child must have lived with the applicants at all times during the one year preceding the application [s.42(4)].

- In cases where a British resident has complied with the relevant requirement and brought a child into the UK for the purposes of adoption, regulation 9 of the Adoptions with a Foreign Element Regulations 2005 requires that the child must have lived with the applicant/s for not less than six months preceding the application.

- In cases where a British resident has not complied with the relevant requirement, the residence requirement is extended to 12 months.

- In any other case, the condition is the child must have lived with the applicant or, in the case of an application by a couple, with one or both of them for not less than three years (continuous or not) during the five years preceding the application [s.42(5)].

- Section 42(4) and (5) does not prevent an application being made if the court gives leave to make it [s.42(6)].

- An adoption order may not be made unless the court is satisfied that sufficient opportunities to see the child at home together with the applicant/s have been given to the adoption agency/local authority.

Reports where child placed by agency [s.43]
- Where an application for an adoption order relates to a child placed for adoption by an adoption agency, the agency must:

  - submit to the court a report on the suitability of applicants and any other matters relevant to the operation of section 1; and

  - assist the court in any manner the court directs.

Notice of intention to adopt [s.44]
- Where a child has not been placed for adoption by an adoption agency, an adoption order may not be made in respect her/him unless the proposed adopters have given notice to the appropriate local authority of their intention to apply for the order ([s.43(2)].

- The notice must be given not more than two years, or less than three months, before the date on which the application for the adoption order is made [s.44(3)].

- Local authority foster carers will require the court's leave to apply if:

  - the child has not lived with them or one of them for a year preceding the application or at least three years within the last five [s.44(4)].

- On receipt of a notice of intention to adopt, the local authority must arrange for the investigation of the matter including, in particular, the suitability of the adopters, and submit to the court a report of the investigation [s.44(5);(6)].

- In particular, the investigation must, so far as practicable, include the suitability of the proposed adopters and any other matters relevant to the operation of section 1 in relation to the application [s.44(6)].

- If a local authority receives a notice of intention to adopt in respect of a child whom it knows was (immediately before the notice was given) looked after by another local authority, it must, within seven days, inform the other local authority [s.44(7)].

- The authority is not to be treated as leaving the child with a person or people as prospective adopters for the purposes of section 18(1)(b), where:

  - a local authority has placed a child with any persons otherwise than as prospective adopters; and

  - the persons give notice of intention to adopt [s.44(8)].

- In section 44, the appropriate local authority is the authority where, at the time of the notice, the proposed adopters have their home. If they do not have a home in England or Wales, regulations make provision as to the relevant local authority.

Suitability of adopters [s.45]
- The Suitability of Adopters Regulations 2005 made under section 9 make provision as to the matters to be taken into account by an adoption agency in determining, or making any report in respect of, the suitability of any persons to adopt a child, in particular, in the case of a couple, proper regard to the need for stability and permanence in their relationship [s.45(1); (2)].

THE MAKING OF ADOPTION ORDERS
Making adoption orders [s.46]
- An adoption order is an order made by the court on an application under section 50 or 51 giving parental responsibility for a child to the adopters or adopter [s.46(1)].

- The making of an adoption order operates to extinguish:

  - the parental responsibility which any person other than the adopters or adopter has for the adopted child immediately before the making of the order;

  - any order under the 1989 Act or the Children (Northern Ireland) Order 1995;

  - any order under the Children (Scotland) Act 1995 other than an excepted order; and

  - any duty arising by virtue of an agreement or an order of a court to make payments, so far as the payments are in respect of the adopted child's maintenance or upbringing for any period after the making of the adoption order, except for an agreement which constitutes a trust, or which expressly provides that the duty is not to be extinguished by the making of an adoption order [s.46(2); (4)].

  'Excepted order' means an order under sections 9, 11(1)(d) or 13 Children (Scotland) Act 1995 or an exclusion order within the meaning of section 76(1) of that Act.

- Section 46(3)(h) preserves the parental status of a parent whose partner obtains an adoption order in respect of her/his child.

- An adoption order may be made even if the child to be adopted is already an adopted child [s.46(5)].

- Before making an adoption order, the court must consider whether there should be arrangements for allowing any person contact with the child; and for that purpose the court must consider any existing or proposed arrangements and obtain any views of the parties to the proceedings [s.46(6)].

Conditions for making adoption orders [s.47]

- If a child has a parent or guardian, an adoption order may not be made unless one of the three conditions described below is met (though s.47 is subject to s.52 – parental etc. consent) [s.47(1)].

- The conditions are related to:

  - consent,

  - placement,

  - orders made in Scotland, Northern Ireland or transitional arrangements.

- The **first condition** is that, in the case of each parent or guardian, the court is satisfied that:

  - the parent or guardian consents to the making of the adoption order;

  - the parent or guardian has consented under section 20 (and has not withdrawn the consent) and does not oppose the making of the adoption order; or

  - the parent's or guardian's consent should be dispensed with [s.47(2)].

  Where she/he has given advance consent under section 20, a parent or guardian may not oppose the making of an adoption order without the court's leave [s.47(3)].

- The **second condition** is that:

  - the child has been placed for adoption by an agency, with the prospective adopters in whose favour the order is proposed to be made; and

  - **either**, the child was placed for adoption with the consent of each parent or guardian and the consent of the mother was given when the child was at least six weeks old, **or** the child was placed for adoption under a placement order; and

- no parent or guardian opposes the making of the adoption order [s.47(4)].

All three of the above requirements must be established to the satisfaction of the court.

■ A parent or guardian may not oppose the making of an adoption order under this second condition without the court's leave [s.47(5)].

■ The **third condition** is that the child is free for adoption by virtue of an order made:

  - in Scotland, under section 18 of the Adoption (Scotland) Act 1978, or

  - in Northern Ireland, under Article 17(1) or 18(1) of the Adoption (Northern Ireland) Order 1987 (S.I. 1987/2203 (N.I. 22) [s.47(6)].

Also, by virtue of transitional provisions (sched. 4, para 7(3)) a freeing order made in England and Wales under the Adoption Act 1976.

The court cannot give leave under section 47(3) or (5) unless satisfied that there has been a change in circumstances since the consent of the parent or guardian was given or, as the case may be, the placement order was made [s.47(7)].

■ An adoption order may not be made in relation to a person who is or has been married [s.47(8)] or has registered a civil partnership.

■ An adoption order may not be made in relation to a person who has attained the age of 19 years [s.47(9)].

Restrictions on making adoption orders [s.48]

■ The court may **not** hear an application for an adoption order, where a previous application for an adoption order in the UK, Isle of Man or any of the Channel Islands, made in relation to the child by the same persons was refused by any court, **unless** it appears to the court that, because of a change in circumstances or for any other reason, it is proper to hear the application.

Applications for adoption: residence and age requirements [s.49]

- A **single** applicant must be domiciled in a part of the British Islands or have been habitually resident there for at least a year preceding the application.

- In the case of **a couple**, either both must have been habitually resident in a part of the British Islands for at least a year or one of them must be domiciled there.

- Applicants for an adoption order must be at least 21 years of age except that a parent adopting her/his own child with her/his partner may be aged 18–20 [s.49(4)].

- References in the ACA 2002 to a child, in connection with any proceedings (whether or not concluded) for adoption e.g. 'child to be adopted' or 'adopted child' include a person who has attained the age of 18 years before the proceedings are concluded [s.49(4)].

Domicile and habitual residence are dealt with in detail in the Adoption Guidance Annex A, paragraphs 1–8.

Adoption by a couple [s.50]

- An application may be made by a couple defined in section 144(4) as:

  • a married couple,

  • civil partners,

  • two people (of different or the same sex) living as partners in an enduring family relationship – other than parent, grandparent, sibling, aunt or uncle.

Adoption by one person [s.51]

- An application can be made by one person if she/he is:

  - unmarried and has not entered into a registered civil partnership;

  - married to or the registered civil partner of the parent of the child; or

  - married and has entered into a civil partnership which has not been dissolved and her/his spouse cannot be found/they have separated and the separation is likely to be permanent/the spouse/partner is by reason of ill-health incapable of making an application.

PLACEMENT AND ADOPTION: GENERAL
Parental etc consent [s.52]

- The court cannot dispense with parental consent to the child being placed for adoption or to the making of an adoption order unless satisfied that:

  - the parent or guardian cannot be found or is incapable of giving consent, or

  - the welfare of the child requires the consent to be dispensed with [s.52(1)].

- 'Consent' means consent given unconditionally and with full understanding of what is involved; but a person may consent to adoption without knowing the identity of the persons in whose favour the order will be made [s.52(5)].

  Any consent given by the mother to the making of an adoption order is ineffective if it is given less than six weeks after her child's birth [s.52(3)].

- 'Parent', except in section 52(9) and section 52(10) below means a parent having parental responsibility.

- The withdrawal of any consent to the placement of a child for adoption, or of any consent given under section 20 is ineffective if it is given after an application for an adoption order is made [s.52(4)].

- Consent must be given in the form prescribed by rules and any withdrawal of consent must also be in the form prescribed by rules, or by notice given to the agency [s.52(7); (8)].

- If an agency has placed a child for adoption under section 19 in pursuance of consent given by a parent of the child, and later, the other parent of the child acquires parental responsibility for her/him:

  - the other parent is to be treated as though she/he had given consent in the same terms in accordance with section 52 [s.52(9); (10)].

Modification of 1989 Act in relation to adoption [s.53]
- Section 53 permits provisions in the Children Act 1989 to be modified in respect of children awaiting adoption – see regulation 45 Adoption Agencies Regulations.

- Where a child is living with a person/persons who have given notice of intention to adopt, parents are not liable to pay any contributions towards the maintenance of the child [Adoption Agencies Regulations reg.45(2)(d)] from the time notice is given until:

  - four months thereafter, or

  - an application for such an order is withdrawn or refused [s.53(5)].

Disclosing information during adoption process [s.54]
- Regulations under section 9 may require adoption agencies in prescribed circumstances to disclose, in accordance with the regulations, information to prospective adopters [s.54(1)].

Disclosure of information

DISCLOSURE OF INFORMATION IN RELATION TO A PERSON'S ADOPTION

Information to be kept about a person's adoption [s.56]

- The Disclosure of Adoption Information (Post-Commencement Adoptions) Regulations 2005 prescribe:

  - the information which an adoption agency must keep in relation to her/his adoption;

  - the form and manner in which it must keep that information;

  - the arrangements for transfer of the information to another adoption agency [s.56(1); (3)].

- Any information kept by an adoption agency by virtue of section 56(1) responsibility (information the agency must keep in relation to a person's adoption) is referred to as 'section 56 information' [s.56(2)].

Restrictions on disclosure of protected etc information [s.57]

- The disclosure of information to a person restricted by virtue of section 57(1) or (2) is referred to as 'protected information' [s.57(3)].

- 'Identifying information' about a person means information which, on its own or together with other information disclosed by an adoption agency, identifies the person or enables the person to be identified [s.57(4)].

- Any 'section 56 information' kept by an adoption agency which is about an adopted or any other person and is or includes identifying information about the person may **only** be disclosed to a person (other than the person the information is about) in accordance with sections 57–65 below [s.57(1)]

- Any information kept by an adoption agency which the agency has obtained from the Registrar General and any other information which would enable the adopted person to obtain a certified copy of her/his birth certificate, or about an entry relating to her/him in the Adoption Contact Register, may only be disclosed to a person by the agency in pursuance of sections 57–65 [s.57(2)].

- Section 57 does not prevent the disclosure of protected information in pursuance of a prescribed agreement to which the adoption agency is a party [s.57(5)].

- Part 3 of The Disclosure of Adoption Information (Post-Commencement Adoptions) Regulations 2005 in defined circumstances authorises an adoption agency to disclose protected information to a person who is not an adopted person [s.57(6)].

DISCLOSURE OF OTHER INFORMATION [s.58]

- Section 58 applies to any section 56 information other than protected information [s.58(1)].

- An adoption agency may, for purposes of its functions, disclose to any person in accordance with prescribed arrangements any information to which section 58 applies [s.58(1)].

- An adoption agency must, in prescribed circumstances, disclose prescribed information to a prescribed person [s.58(2)].

Offence [s.59]

- Regulation 21 of the Disclosure of Adoption Information (Post-Commencement Adoptions) Regulations 2005 provides that a registered adoption society which discloses any information in contravention of section 57 is guilty of an offence and liable on summary conviction to a fine not exceeding level 5 on the standard scale [s.59(1)].

Disclosing information to an adopted adult [s.60]

■ Section 60 applies to an adopted person who has attained the age of 18 years [s.60(1)].

■ The adopted person has the right, at her/his request, to receive from the appropriate adoption agency:

- any information which would enable her/him to obtain a certified copy of the record of her/his birth, unless the High Court orders otherwise, and

- any prescribed information disclosed to the adopters by the agency by virtue of section 54 [s.60(2)].

■ The High Court may make an order under the former of the two section 60(2) provisions, on an application by the appropriate adoption agency, if satisfied that the circumstances are exceptional [s.60(3)].

■ The adopted person also has the right, at her/his request, to receive from the court which made the adoption order a copy of any prescribed document or prescribed order relating to the adoption [s.60(4)].

Section 60(4) does not apply to a document or order so far as it contains information which is protected information [s.60(5)].

Disclosing protected information about adults [s.61]

■ Section 61 applies where:

- a person applies to the appropriate adoption agency for protected information to be disclosed to her/him, and

- **none** of the information is about a person who is a child at the time of the application [s.61(1)].

■ The agency is not required to proceed with the application unless it considers it appropriate to do so [s.61(2)].

- If the agency does proceed, it must take all reasonable steps to obtain the views of any person the information is about as to the disclosure of the information [s.61(3)].

- The agency may then disclose the information if it considers it appropriate to do so [s.61(4)].

- In deciding if it is appropriate to proceed with the application or disclose the information, the agency must consider:

  - the welfare of the adopted person;

  - any views obtained under section 61(3);

  - any prescribed matters; and

  - all other circumstances of the case [s.61(5)]

- Section 61 does not apply to a request by the adopted person for information to enable a certified copy of her/his birth certificate, to prescribed information disclosed to her/his adopters nor to the disclosure of protected information which the agency is required by regulations to disclose [s.61(6)].

Disclosing protected information about children [s.62]
- Section 62 applies where:

  - a person applies to the appropriate adoption agency for protected information to be disclosed to her/him, and

  - **any** of the information is about a person who is a child at the time of the application [s.62(1)].

- The agency is not required to proceed with the application unless it considers it appropriate to do so and if it does proceed, then, so far as the information is about a child, the agency must take all reasonable steps to obtain, the views of:

- any parent or guardian of the child, and

- the child, if the agency considers it appropriate to do so having regard to her/his age and understanding and to all the other circumstances of the case [s.62(2); (3)].

So far as the information is about a person who has at the time attained the age of 18 years, the agency must take all reasonable steps to obtain her/his views as to the disclosure of the information [s.62(4)].

■ The agency may then disclose the information if it considers it appropriate to do so [s.62(5)].

■ In deciding if it is appropriate to proceed with the application, or disclose the information, where any of the information is about a person who is at the time a child:

- if the child is an adopted child, the child's welfare must be the paramount consideration,

- in the case of any other child, the agency must have particular regard to the child's welfare [s.62(6)].

In deciding whether it is appropriate to proceed with the application or disclose the information, the agency must consider the welfare of the adopted person when she/he is not a child), any views obtained under section 62(3) or (4), any prescribed matters and all the other circumstances of the case [s.62(7)].

Counselling [s.63]
■ Part 5 of the Disclosure of Adoption Information (Post-Commencement Adoptions) Regulations 2005 requires adoption agencies to give information about availability of counselling to persons:

- seeking information from them;

- considering objecting or consenting to the disclosure of information by the agency in pursuance of this group of sections; or

- considering entering with the agency into an agreement [s.63(1)].

Other provision to be made by regulations [s.64]
- The Disclosure of Adoption Information (Post-Commencement Adoptions) Regulations 2005 make detailed provision for the purposes of sections 57–65 (disclosure of information).

Status of adopted children

Meaning of adoption [s.66]
- In sections 66–76 'adoption' means (and related expressions should be interpreted accordingly):

- an adoption by an adoption order or a Scottish or Northern Irish adoption order;

- an adoption by an order made in the Isle of Man or any of the Channel Islands;

- an adoption effected under the law of a Convention country outside the British Islands, certified in pursuance of Article 23(1) of the Convention (referred to as a 'Convention adoption');

- an overseas adoption (s.87); or

- an adoption recognised by the law of England and Wales and effected under the law of any other country [s.66(1)].

- References in sections 66–76 to 'adoption' exclude pre-commencement adoptions [s.66(2)].

Any reference in an enactment to an adopted person within the meaning of these sections includes a reference to an adopted child within the meaning of Part 4 Adoption Act 1976 (this part of the 1976 Act being preserved by Schedule 5 of this Act) [s.66(3)].

Status conferred by adoption [s.67]

■ An adopted person is to be treated in law as if born to the adopter/s [s.67(1)].

■ An adopted person is the **legitimate** child of the adopter/s and must be treated as the child of their relationship if adopted by:

  • a couple, or

  • one of a couple under section 51(2) i.e. where the person has attained 21 and is the partner of the parent of the child [s.67(2)].

■ If adopted by one member of a couple under section 51(2), a child must be treated in law as the child of the couple's relationship (though this does not affect any reference in this Act to her/his natural parent or other natural relationship) [s.67(3)(a)].

■ In any other case, section 67(3)(b) provides that an adopted person must in law be treated **only** as the child of the adopter/s, though once again this does not affect any reference in this Act to a child's natural parent or other natural relationship.

■ Where an adopter is a sole adopter **and** the natural parent, section 67(3)(b) has no effect with respect to anything that depends upon the child's relationship to that parent, e.g. entitlement to property [s.67(4)].

Section 67 takes effect from the date of the adoption [s.67(5)].

Adoptive relatives [s.68]

■ A relationship existing by virtue of section 67 may be referred to as an adoptive relationship, and:

- an adopter may be referred to as an adoptive parent/adoptive father/adoptive mother; and

- any other relative of any degree under an adoptive relationship may be referred to as an adoptive relative of that degree [s.68(1)].

■ If a child was adopted by a couple of the same sex, or a partner of the child's parent, where the couple are of the same sex:

- a reference to the adoptive 'mother' and 'father' of a child is to be read as a reference to the child's adoptive parents [s.68(3)].

The Registers

ADOPTED CHILDREN REGISTER ETC
Adoptive relatives [s.77]

■ The Registrar General must maintain the Adopted Children Register, which is not open to public inspection or search [s.77(1); (2)].

■ No entries may be made in the Adopted Children Register other than entries:

- directed to be made in it by adoption orders, or

- required to be made under Schedule 1 [s.77(3)].

■ A certified copy of an entry in the Register, if purporting to be sealed or stamped with the seal of the General Register Office, is sufficient evidence of the adoption to which it relates [s.77(4)].

■ Where an entry in the Register contains a record of the date of birth, country, or district and sub-district, of the birth of the adopted person:

- a certified copy of the entry is also sufficient evidence in all respects as if the copy were a certified copy of an entry in the registers of live births [s.77(5)].

Searches and copies [s.78]

■ The Registrar General must continue to maintain an index of the Adopted Children Register [s.78(1)].

■ Any person may:

  • search the index, and

  • have a certified copy of any entry in the Adopted Children Register [s.78(2)].

■ A person is not entitled to have a certified copy of an entry in that Register relating to an adopted person who has not attained the age of 18 years unless she/he has provided the Registrar General with the prescribed particulars.

'Prescribed' means prescribed by regulations made by the Registrar General with the approval of the Chancellor of the Exchequer [s.78(3)].

Connection between the register and birth records [s.79]

■ The Registrar General must make traceable the connection between any entry in the registers of live births or other records which has been marked 'Adopted' and any corresponding entry in the Adopted Children Register [s.79(1)].

■ Information kept by the Registrar General for the above is not open to public inspection or search [s.79(2)].

■ Any such information, and any other information which would enable an adopted person to obtain a certified copy of the record of her/his birth, may **only** be disclosed by the Registrar General in accordance with section 79 [s.79(3)].

- In relation to a person adopted before 30.12.05, the court may, in exceptional circumstances, order the Registrar General to give any information mentioned in section 79(3) to a person [s.79(4)].

- On an application made in the prescribed manner by the appropriate adoption agency in respect of an adopted person, a record of whose birth is kept by the Registrar General, the Registrar General must give the agency any information relating to the adopted person which is mentioned in section 79(3) [s.79(5)].

  'Appropriate adoption agency' has the same meaning as in section 65. In relation to a person adopted before 30.12.05, Schedule 2 applies instead of section 79(5).

- On an application made in the prescribed manner by an adopted person, a record of whose birth is kept by the Registrar General and who is under the age of 18 years, and intends to be married or enter into a civil partnership:

  • the Registrar General must inform the applicant if it appears from information contained in the registers of live births or other records that the applicant and the person whom the applicant intends to marry or enter into a civil partnership with, may be within the prohibited degrees of relationship for the purposes of the Marriage Act 1949 [s.79(7)].

- Before the Registrar General gives any information by virtue of this section, any prescribed fee which he has demanded must be paid [s.79(8)].

Adoption Contact Register [s.80]

- The Registrar General must continue to maintain at the General Register Office, in accordance with regulations, a register in two Parts, to be called the Adoption Contact Register [s.80(1)].

- Part 1 of the register is to contain information about adopted persons who have given notice expressing their wishes as to making contact with their relatives [s.80(2)].

- The Registrar General may only make an entry in Part 1 of the register for an adopted person who:

  - has a birth record kept by the Registrar General;

  - has attained the age of 18 years; and

  - who the Registrar General is satisfied has such information as is necessary to enable her/him to obtain a certified copy of the birth certificate [s.80(3)].

- Part 2 is to contain prescribed information about persons who have given notice expressing their wishes, as relatives of adopted persons, as to making contact with those persons [s.80(4)].

- The Registrar General may only make an entry in Part 2 of the register for a person who:

  - has attained the age of 18 years, and

  - the Registrar General is satisfied is a relative of an adopted person and has such information as is necessary to enable her/him to obtain a certified copy of the record of the adopted person's birth.

- Regulations provide for:

  - the disclosure of information contained in one Part of the register to persons for whom there is an entry in the other Part, and

  - the payment of prescribed fees [s.80(6)].

Adoption Contact Register: supplementary [s.81]
- The Adoption Contact Register is not to be open to public inspection or search [s.81(1)].

- In section 80, 'relative', in relation to an adopted person, means any person who (but for her/his adoption) would be related to her/him by blood (including half-blood) or marriage [s.81(2)].

■ The Registrar General must not give any information entered in the register to any person except in accordance with section 80(6)(a) or regulations.

Adoptions with a foreign element

BRINGING CHILDREN INTO AND OUT OF THE UK
Restrictions on bringing children in [s.83]
■ Section 83 applies where a person habitually resident in the British Islands – a 'British resident' – alone or jointly with another person:

• brings, or causes another to bring, a child habitually resident outside the British Islands into the UK for the purpose of adoption by the British resident; or

• at any time brings, or causes another to bring, into the UK a child adopted by the British resident under an external adoption effected within the previous six months [s.83(1)].

Section 83 does not apply if the child is intended to be adopted under a Convention adoption order [s.83(2)].

■ An 'external' adoption means an adoption, other than a Convention adoption, of a child effected under the law of any country or territory outside the British Islands, whether or not the adoption is:

• an adoption within the meaning of Chapter 4, or

• a full adoption (within the meaning of section 88(3)) [s.83(3)].

■ For regulations, see The Adoptions with a Foreign Element Regulations 2005.

■ If a person brings, or causes another to bring, a child into the UK at any time in circumstances where section 83 applies, she/he is guilty of an offence if, before that time, or before any later time prescribed in the regulations:

- she/he has not complied with any requirement or conditions imposed by those regulations [s.83(7)]

■ A person guilty of an offence under section 83 is liable:

- on summary conviction to imprisonment for a term not exceeding six months, or a fine not exceeding the statutory maximum, or both;

- on conviction on indictment, to imprisonment for a term not exceeding 12 months, or a fine, or both [s.83(8)].

Giving parental responsibility prior to adoption abroad [s.84]
■ The High Court may, on an application by persons who the court is satisfied intend to adopt a child under the law of a country or territory outside the British Islands, make an order giving parental responsibility for the child to them [s.84(1)].

■ An order under section 84 may not give parental responsibility to persons who the court is satisfied meet those requirements as to domicile, or habitual residence, in England and Wales which have to be met if an adoption order is to be made in favour of those persons [s.84(2)].

■ An order under section 84 may not be made unless the requirements prescribed by regulation 10, the Adoptions with a Foreign Element Regulations 2005, are satisfied [s.84(3)].

■ An application for an order under section 84 may not be made unless at all times during the preceding 10 weeks the child's home was with the applicant or, in the case of an application by two people, both of them [s.84(4)].

- Section 46(2)–(4) has effect in relation to an order under section 84 as it has effect in relation to adoption orders [s.84(5)].

- Regulation 11 of the Adoptions with a Foreign Element Regulations 2005 provides for any provision of this Act which refers to adoption orders to apply, with or without modifications, to orders under section 84 [s.84(6)].

Restrictions on taking children out of the UK [s.85]
- A child who is a Commonwealth citizen, or is habitually resident in the UK, must not be removed from the UK to a place outside the British Islands for the purpose of adoption unless the prospective adopters have parental responsibility for the child by virtue of an order under section 84, or she/he is removed under the authority of an order under section 49 Adoption (Scotland) Act 1978 or Article 57 Adoption (Northern Ireland) Order 1987 [s.85(1); (2)].

- Removing a child from the UK includes arranging to do so, and the circumstances in which a person arranges to remove a child from the UK include those where she/he:

  - enters into an arrangement or initiates or takes part in any negotiations for that purpose, or

  - causes another person to take any step mentioned in either of the above paragraphs [s.85(3)].

- A person who removes a child from the UK in contravention of section 85(1) is guilty of an offence [s.85(4)].

- A person is not guilty of an offence under section 85(4) of causing a person to take any step mentioned in the first or second paragraphs of section 85(3) unless it is proved that she/he knew or had reason to suspect the step taken would contravene section 85(1).

- A person guilty of an offence under section 85 is liable:

- on summary conviction to imprisonment for a term not exceeding six months, or a fine not exceeding the statutory maximum, or both;

- on conviction on indictment, to imprisonment for a term not exceeding 12 months, or a fine, or both [s.85(6)].

Power to modify sections 83 and 85 [s.86]

■ Regulations under section 86 (not yet made) may provide for section 83 (restrictions on bringing a child into the UK) to not apply if (as well as satisfying specified conditions) adopters/prospective adopters are natural parents, natural relatives or guardians of the child in question or if the British resident in question is a partner of a parent of the child [s.86(1)].

■ Regulations (not yet made) may also provide for section 85(1) (restriction on taking child out of the UK) to apply with modifications, or not to apply, if (as well as any prescribed conditions being met) the prospective adopters are parents, relatives or guardians of the child in question (or one of them is), or the prospective adopter is a partner of a parent of the child.

OVERSEAS ADOPTIONS
Overseas adoptions [s.87]

■ In this Act, 'overseas adoption':

- means an adoption of a description specified in an order made by the Secretary of State, being a description of adoptions effected under the law of any country or territory outside the British Islands, but

- does not include a Convention adoption [s.86(1)].

Annulment etc of overseas or Hague Convention adoptions [s.89]

■ Section 89 enables the High Court to:

- annul a Convention adoption or Convention adoption order on the grounds the adoption is contrary to public policy;

- by order provide for an overseas adoption or a determination under section 91 (overseas determinations and orders) to cease to be valid;

- decide the extent, if any, to which a determination under section 91 has been affected by a subsequent determination under that section;

- decide that an overseas adoption or a determination under section 91 is to be treated as invalid (if contrary to public policy or because the authority which purported to authorise it was not competent to do so).

Miscellaneous provisions

RESTRICTIONS
Restriction on arranging adoptions etc [s.92]

- A person who is neither an adoption agency nor acting in pursuance of an order of the High Court must not take any of the following steps:

  - asking a person other than an adoption agency to provide a child for adoption;

  - asking a person other than an adoption agency to provide prospective adopters for a child;

  - offering to find a child for adoption;

  - offering a child for adoption to a person other than an adoption agency;

  - handing over a child to any person other than an adoption agency with a view to the child's adoption by that or another person;

  - receiving a child handed over to her/him in contravention of the paragraph immediately above;

  - entering into an agreement with any person for the adoption of a child, or for the purpose of facilitating the adoption of a child, where no adoption agency is acting on behalf of the child in the adoption;

  - initiating or taking part in negotiations of which the purpose is the conclusion of an agreement within the paragraph immediately above;

- causing another person to take any of the steps mentioned in the preceding eight paragraphs.

■ **If** the prospective adopters are parents, relatives or guardians of the child (or one of them is), or the prospective adopter is the partner of a parent of the child, she/he is **not** prohibited from:

- offering a child for adoption to a person other than an adoption agency;

- handing over a child to any person other than an adoption agency with a view to the child's adoption by that or another person;

- entering into an agreement with any person for the child's adoption or facilitation of adoption, where no agency is acting on behalf of the child;

- initiating or taking part in negotiations in order to conclude the above agreement;

- causing another person to take any of the above steps.

Offence of breaching restrictions under section 92 [s.93]

■ If a person contravenes section 92(1), she/he is guilty of an offence and, if that person is an adoption society, the person who manages the society is also guilty of the offence [s.93(1)].

■ A person is not guilty of receiving a child handed over to her/him for adoption unless it is proved that she/he knew or had reason to suspect that this was the case.

■ A person is not guilty of an offence of causing a person to take any of the prohibited steps of section 91(2) unless it is proved that she/he knew or had reason to suspect she/he would be doing so.

A person guilty of an offence under section 93 is liable on summary conviction to imprisonment for a term not exceeding six months, or a fine not exceeding £10,000, or both [s.93(5)].

Restrictions on reports [s.94]

■ The Restriction on Preparations of Adoption Reports Regulations 2005 make it clear that only a registered and suitably qualified social worker may prepare a report for any person about the suitability of a child for adoption or of a person to adopt a child or about the adoption, or placement for adoption, of a child [s.94(1)].

■ A person is guilty of an offence if she/he:

- contravenes section 94(1), or

- causes a person to prepare a report, or submits to any person a report which has been prepared, in contravention of that subsection [s.94(2)].

■ The person who manages the society is also guilty of the offence if a person who works for an adoption society:

- contravenes section 94(1), or

- causes a person to prepare a report, or submits to any person a report which has been prepared, in contravention of that subsection [s.94(2)].

■ A person is not guilty of an offence under section 94(2) (causing a person to prepare a report, etc.) unless it is proved she/he knew or had reason to suspect that the report would be, or had been, prepared in contravention of section 94(1) [s.94(4)].

■ A person guilty of an offence under section 94 is liable on summary conviction to imprisonment for a term not exceeding six months, or a fine not exceeding level 5 on the standard scale, or both [s.94(5)].

Prohibition of certain payments [s.95]

■ Section 95 applies to any payment (other than an excepted payment) which is made for or in consideration of:

- the adoption of a child;

- giving any consent required in connection with the adoption of a child;

- removing from the UK a child who is a Commonwealth citizen, or is habitually resident in the UK, to a place outside the British Islands for the purpose of adoption;

- a person (who is neither an adoption agency nor acting in pursuance of an order of the High Court) taking any step mentioned in section 92(2);

- preparing, causing to be prepared or submitting a report, preparation of which contravenes section 94(1) [s.95(1)].

■ A person is guilty of an offence and liable on summary conviction to imprisonment for up to six months, a fine not exceeding £10,000 or both [s.95(4)] if she/he:

- makes any payment to which section 95 applies;

- agrees or offers to make any such payment; or

- receives or agrees to receive or attempts to obtain any such payment [s.95(3)]

Excepted payments [s.96]
■ A payment is an 'excepted' one if it is made:

- by virtue of, or in accordance with, provisions of this Act, the Adoption (Scotland) Act 1978 or the Adoption (Northern Ireland) Order 1987 [s.96(1)];

- to a registered adoption society in respect of expenses reasonably incurred by the society in connection with the adoption/proposed adoption of a child, by a parent or guardian of a child, or person who adopts or proposes to adopt a child [s.96(2)];

- in respect of any legal or medical expenses incurred or to be incurred by any person in connection with an application to a court which she/he has made/proposes to make for an adoption order, a placement order, or an order under section 26 or section 84 [s.96(3)];

- for removing from the UK a child who is a Commonwealth citizen or habitually resident in the UK, to a place outside the British Islands for the purpose of adoption so long as the condition in section 85(2) is met (prospective adopters have parental responsibility and authorisation in relevant Scottish or Northern Irish law), and payment is for travel and accommodation expenses reasonably incurred in removing the child from the UK for the purpose of adoption [s.96(4)].

INFORMATION
Pre-commencement adoptions: information [s.98]

- The Adoption Information and Intermediary Services (Pre-Commencement Adoptions) Regulations 2005 make provision for the purpose of:

  - assisting persons adopted before the appointed day who have attained the age of 18 to obtain information in relation to their adoption; and

  - facilitating contact between such persons and their relatives [s.98(1)].

- For that purpose the regulations may confer functions on:

  - registered adoption support agencies;

  - the Registrar General; and

  - adoption agencies [s.98(2)].

Appeals [s.94 Children Act 1989 as amended by s.100]

- An appeal must be made to the High Court against:

  - the making by a Magistrates' Court of any order under the Children Act 1989 or Adoption and Children Act 2002;

  - any refusal by a Magistrates' Court to make such an order.

Proceedings under the Adoption and Children Act 2002 in the High Court or a County Court may be heard and determined in private [s.101].

THE CHILDREN AND FAMILY COURT ADVISORY AND SUPPORT SERVICE (CAFCASS)
Officers of the service [s.102]

- Rules must provide for the appointment of an officer of the Children and Family Court Advisory and Support Service ('the Service') for the purposes of:

  - any relevant application;

  - signification by any person of any consent to placement or adoption [s.102(1)].

- A report prepared in pursuance of the rules on matters relating to the welfare of a child must:

  - deal with prescribed matters (unless the court orders otherwise); and

  - be made in the manner required by the court [s.102(4)].

- A CAFCASS officer must not be appointed under section 102 if she/he:

  - is employed by the local authority which made the application (application for the making, varying or revocation of a placement order);

  - is employed by the adoption agency which placed the child (application for an adoption order in respect of a child placed for adoption); or

  - is within a description prescribed by the above rules [s.102(5)].

Rights of officers of the service to have access to adoption agency records [s.103]

- Where a CAFCASS officer has been appointed to act under section 102(1), she/he has the right at all reasonable times to examine and take copies of any records of, or held by, an adoption agency compiled in connection with the making, or proposed making, by any person of any application under this Part in respect of the child concerned [s.103(1)].

- Where the officer takes a copy of any record which she/he is entitled to examine under section 103, that copy or any part of it is admissible as evidence of any matter referred to in any:

  - report she/he makes to the court in the proceedings or

  - evidence which she/he gives [s.103(2)].

EVIDENCE
Evidence of consent [s.104]

- If a document signifying any required consent is witnessed in accordance with rules, it is admissible in evidence without further proof of the signature of the person by whom it was executed [s.104(1)].

  A document signifying any such witnessed consent is presumed to be valid unless the contrary is proved [s.104(2)].

Avoiding delay [s.109]

- In proceedings in which a question may arise as to whether an adoption order or placement order should be made, or any other question with respect to such an order, the court must (in the light of any rules made by virtue of section 109(2)):

  - draw up a timetable with a view to determining such a question without delay; and

  - give such directions as it considers appropriate for the purpose of ensuring that the timetable is adhered to [s.109(1)].

Service of notices etc [s.104]

- Any notice or information required to be given by virtue of this Act may be given by post [s.110].

Special guardianship [s.14A–G Children Act 1989 introduced by s.115]

■ This section summarises what is (for purposes of adoption-related work) the most significant amendment made by the ACA 2002 to the Children Act 1989, i.e. the introduction of 'special guardianship' via section 115.

Other amendments to the Children Act e.g. changes to allocation of parental responsibility, application for section 8 orders by foster carers, extension of residence orders to 18, representation procedures, review of cases, advocacy, definition of harm and children's interests in proceedings are not covered in this guide.

Purpose of special guardianship order

■ Special guardianship orders are intended to meet the needs of children who cannot live with their birth parents, for whom adoption is not appropriate but who could still benefit from a legally secure placement.

Definition and conditions for making special guardianship order [s.14A Children Act 1989]

■ A 'special guardianship order' is an order appointing one or more individuals to be a child's 'special guardian' (or special guardians) [s.14A (1) Children Act 1989].

■ A special guardian must:

• be aged 18 or over and

• not be a parent of the child in question [s.14A(2) Children Act 1989].

■ The court may make a special guardianship order with respect to any child on the application of an individual (or joint application of more than one such individual – couples need not be married) who:

• is/are entitled to make such an application with respect to the child; or

- has/have obtained the leave of the court to make the application [s.14A(3) Children Act 1989].

A person who is, or was at any time within the last six months, a local authority foster carer of a child may not apply for a special guardianship order with respect to that child unless she/he has the authority's consent, is a relative or the child has lived with her/him for a total of at least one year preceding the application [effect of s.14A(4) Children Act 1989].

Eligibility to make an application for special guardianship order [s.14A(5)–(7) Children Act 1989]

- The individuals who are entitled to apply for a special guardianship order with respect to a child are:

  - any guardian of the child;

  - any individual in whose favour a residence order is in force with respect to the child;

  - any person with whom the child has lived for at least three years (in the period three months to five years before the application is made);

  - where a residence order is in force with respect to the child, any person who has consent of those persons in whose favour the residence order was made;

  - where the child is in the care of the local authority, any person who has the consent of that authority;

  - any person who has the consent of each of those (if any) who have parental responsibility for the child;

  - a local authority foster carer with whom the child has lived for a period of at least one year immediately preceding the application [s.14A(5) Children Act 1989].

- The court may also make a special guardianship order with respect to a child in any family proceedings (adoption proceedings are family proceedings) in which a question arises with respect to the welfare of the child if:

- an application for the order has been made by an individual (or more than one such individual jointly) who is entitled to or has obtained the court's leave to do so;

- the court considers that a special guardianship order should be made even though no such application has been made [s.14A(6) Children Act 1989].

■ No individual may make an application under section 14A(3) or (6) unless she/he has given three months' written notice of her/his intention to make the application:

- if the child in question is being looked after by a local authority, to that local authority; or

- otherwise, to the local authority in whose area the individual is ordinarily resident [s.14A(7) Children Act 1989].

Response to application for special guardianship order [s.14A (8)–(13) Children Act 1989]

■ On receipt of such a notice, the local authority must investigate the matter and prepare a report for the court.

■ The court may itself ask a local authority to conduct such an investigation and prepare such a report, and the local authority must do so [s.14A(8); (9) Children Act 1989].

The local authority may make such arrangements as it sees fit for any person to act on its behalf in connection with conducting an investigation or preparing a report referred to in section 14A(8) or (9) [s.14A(10) Children Act 1989].

■ The court may not make a special guardianship order unless it has received a report dealing with the matters referred to in section 14A(8) [s.14A(11) Children Act 1989].

- Where a person applies for leave to make an application for a special guardianship order, the court, in deciding whether to grant leave, must have particular regard to:

  - the nature of the proposed application;

  - the applicant's connection with the child;

  - any risk there might be of that proposed application disrupting the child's life to such an extent that she/he would be harmed by it; and

  - (where she/he is looked after by a local authority) the authority's plans for the child's future and the wishes and feelings of the child's parents [s.14A(12) Children Act 1989].

  When a placement order is in force, no special guardianship order may be made in respect of a child unless an application has been made for an adoption order and the applicant for the guardianship order has obtained the court's leave under section 29(5) or (if she/he is a guardian of the child) has obtained the court's leave under section 47(5). Where leave has been given, the requirement for three months' notice in section 14A(7) applications does not apply [effect of s.14A(13) Children Act 1989].

  Making a special guardianship order [s.14B Children Act 1989]
- Before making a special guardianship order, the court must consider whether, if the order were made:

  - a contact order should also be made with respect to the child; and

  - any section 8 order in force with respect to the child should be varied or discharged [s.14B(1) Children Act 1989].

- On making a special guardianship order, the court may also:

- give leave for the child to be known by a new surname;

- grant the leave required by section 14C(3)(b), either generally or for specified purposes [s.14B(2) Children Act 1989].

Effect of a special guardianship order [s.14C Children Act 1989]

■ The effect of a special guardianship order is that while the order remains in force:

- a special guardian appointed by the order has parental responsibility for the child in respect of whom it is made; and

- subject to any other order in force with respect to the child under the Children Act, is entitled to exercise parental responsibility to the exclusion of any other person with parental responsibility for the child (apart from another special guardian) [s.14C(1) Children Act 1989].

■ A special guardian is **not** entitled to provide consent to key decisions where statute or case law require the consent of more than one person with parental responsibility in a matter affecting the child e.g.:

- sterilisation/circumcision;

- adoption or placement for adoption.

■ While a special guardianship order is in force with respect to a child, no person may (without either the written consent of every person who has parental responsibility for the child or the leave of the court):

- cause the child to be known by a new surname; or

- remove her/him from the UK [s.14C(3) Children Act 1989].

The child's special guardian is allowed to remove the child from the UK for a period of less than three months [s.14C(4) Children Act 1989].

■ If the child with respect to whom a special guardianship order is in force dies, her/his special guardian must take reasonable steps to give notice of that fact to each:

- parent of the child with parental responsibility, and

- guardian of the child.

If the child has more than one special guardian, and one has taken such steps in relation to a particular parent or guardian, any other special guardian need not also do so [s.14C(5) Children Act 1989].

Variation and discharge of a special guardianship order [s.14D Children Act 1989]

■ The court may vary or discharge a special guardianship order on the application of:

- the special guardian (or any of them, if there are more than one);

- any parent or guardian of the child concerned;

- any individual in whose favour a residence order is in force with respect to the child;

- any individual not falling into the above categories, who has, or immediately before the making of the special guardianship order had, parental responsibility for the child;

- the child her/himself; or

- a local authority designated in a care order with respect to the child [s.14D(1) Children Act 1989].

■ In any family proceedings in which a question arises with respect to the welfare of a child with respect to whom a special guardianship order is in force, the court may also vary or discharge the special guardianship order if it considers that the order should be varied or discharged, even though no application has been made under section 14D(1) [s.14D(2) Children Act 1989].

- Under section 14D(3), the following must obtain the leave of the court before making an application under section 14D(1):

  - the child;

  - any parent or guardian of her/him;

  - any step-parent who has acquired, and has not lost, parental responsibility for the child by virtue of section 4A;

  - any individual (other than special guardian, parent or guardian or person in whose favour a residence order is in force) who immediately before the making of the special guardianship order had, but no longer has, parental responsibility for her/him.

- Where the person applying for leave to make an application under section 14D(1) is the child, the court may only grant leave if it is satisfied that she/he has sufficient understanding to make the proposed application [s.14D(4) Children Act 1989].

- The court may not grant leave to a person (other than the child) under section 14D(3) unless it is satisfied that there has been a significant change in circumstances since the making of the special guardianship order [s.14D(5) Children Act 1989].

Special guardianship order: Supplementary provisions [s.14E Children Act 1989]

- In proceedings in which any question of making, varying or discharging a special guardianship order arises, the court shall (in the light of any rules made by virtue of 14E(3)):

  - draw up a timetable with a view to determining the question without delay; and

  - give such directions as it considers appropriate for the purpose of ensuring, so far as is reasonably practicable, that the timetable is adhered to [s.14E(1) Children Act 1989].

Section 14E(1) applies also in relation to proceedings in which any other question with respect to a special guardianship order arises. A special guardianship order, or an order varying one, may contain provisions which are to have effect for a specified period [s.14E(4) Children Act 1989].

Special guardianship order: support services [s.14F Children Act 1989]

■ Each local authority must make arrangements for the provision within their area of special guardianship support services i.e.:

- counselling, advice and information, and

- such other services as are prescribed [s.14F(1) Children Act 1989].

■ At the request of any of the following persons, a local authority may carry out an assessment of that person's needs for special guardianship support services:

- a child with respect to whom a special guardianship order is in force;

- a special guardian;

- a parent.

The regulations provide for the circumstances in which a local authority *must* comply with a report for assessment.

■ A local authority may, at the request of any other person, carry out an assessment of that person's needs for special guardianship support services [s.14F(4) Children Act 1989].

■ Where, as a result of an assessment, a local authority decides that a person has needs for special guardianship support services, it must then decide whether to provide any such services to that person [s.14F(5) Children Act 1989].

■ The local authority must prepare a plan in accordance with which special guardianship support services are to be provided to the person and keep the plan under review, **if**:

- the local authority decides to provide any special guardianship support services to a person; and
- the circumstances fall within a prescribed description [s.14F(6) Children Act 1989].

■ A local authority may provide special guardianship support services (or any part of them) by securing their provision by:

- another local authority; or
- a person as defined in the Special Guardianship Regulations 2005.

A local authority may also arrange with any such authority or person for that other authority or that person to carry out the local authority's functions in relation to assessments under section 14.

■ A local authority may carry out an assessment of the needs of any person for the purposes of special guardianship at the same time as an assessment of her/his needs is made under any other provision of the Children Act or under any other enactment [s.14F(10) Children Act 1989].

■ Section 27 (co-operation between authorities) applies in relation to the exercise of functions of a local authority introduced by section 115 as it applies in relation to the exercise of functions of a local authority under Part 3 [s.14F(11) Children Act 1989].

Special guardianship order support services: representations [s.14G Children Act 1989]

■ Every local authority shall establish a procedure for considering representations (including complaints) made to it by any person to whom it may provide special guardianship support services about the discharge of its functions under section 1F in relation to her/him [s.14G(1) Children Act 1989].

- Regulations may be made by the Secretary of State imposing time limits on the making of the above representations [s.14G(2) Children Act 1989].

Advertisements and Adoption & Children Act Register

- This section summarises provisions relating to:

  • advertisements in the UK; and

  • the Adoption and Children Act Register.

ADVERTISEMENTS IN THE UK
Restriction on advertisements etc [s.123]
- A person must not publish or distribute an advertisement or information or cause such an advertisement or information to be published or distributed indicating that:

  • the parent or guardian of a child wants the child to be adopted;

  • a person wants to adopt a child;

  • a person other than an adoption agency is willing to make any of the arrangements specified in section 92(2);

  • a person other than an adoption agency is willing to receive a child handed over to her/him with a view to the child's adoption by him or another; or

  • a person is willing to remove a child from the UK for the purposes of adoption.

- Section 123 applies to information about how to do anything which would constitute an offence under the Adoption (Scotland) Act 1978, the Adoption (Northern Ireland) Order 1987 (whether or not the information includes a warning that doing the thing in question may constitute an offence) or information about a particular child as a child available for adoption.

- Publishing or distributing an advertisement or information means publishing it or distributing it to the public and includes doing so by electronic means (for example, by means of the internet), and the public includes selected members of the public as well as the public generally or any section of the public.

Section 123(1) does not apply to publication or distribution by or on behalf of an adoption agency [s.123(5)].

- References to an adoption agency in section 123 include a prescribed person outside the UK exercising functions corresponding to those of an adoption agency, if the functions are being exercised in prescribed circumstances.

In this section 'adoption agency' includes a Scottish or Northern Irish adoption agency, references to adoption are to the adoption of persons, wherever they may be habitually resident, effected under the law of any country or territory, whether within or outside the British Islands [s.123(9)].

Offence of breaching restriction under section 123 [s.124]

- A person who contravenes section 123(1) is guilty of an offence [s.124(1)] but a person is not guilty of an offence under section 124 unless it is proved she/he knew or had reason to suspect that section 123 applied to the advertisement or information [s.124(2)].

A person guilty of an offence under section 124 is liable on summary conviction to imprisonment for a term not exceeding three months, or a fine not exceeding level 5 on the standard scale, or both [s.124(3)].

ADOPTION AND CHILDREN ACT REGISTER
Adoption and Children Act Register [s.125]

- These provisions of the Act have not been brought into force, but the National Adoption Register continues to function under an administrative arrangement between the Secretary of State and the contracting agency, currently BAAF.

Part II

Regulations

Adoption Agencies Regulations 2005

- These Regulations apply in England only and govern the operation and duties of adoption agencies.

Panel
Although there is no requirement to consider permanent fostering plans or matches, a joint adoption and permanence panel can help reduce delay for children. However, such a panel, if it also makes recommendations on approval of foster carers, must comply with these regulations and the Fostering Services Regulations 2002 [Guidance Annex B 7–11].

- Agencies must have at least one adoption panel, membership (not exceeding 10) to include:

  - an independent Chair;

  - two suitably experienced social workers;

  - an elected member (local authority) or director/manager (voluntary agency);

  - a medical adviser;

  - three independent members.

Independent Chair means not within the last year a trustee (voluntary agency), member (local authority agency) or employee of the local authority's children and family service, or related to such a person. Independent member means not in the last year a trustee or employee, or related to an employee (voluntary agency); or a member of the local authority or employee of its children and family service, or related to such an employee; or an adopter approved by the agency or with a child placed by the agency, unless it is more than 12 months since the adoption order.

'Related to' includes by marriage or civil partnership and as members of the same household.

Agencies should ensure a gender balance and that the membership reflects the composition of the community [Guidance 1.15 & 16].

- One member is to be appointed by the agency as Vice-chair.

- With the exception of the medical adviser (who may hold office indefinitely), members may serve for up to three terms of three years.

  Special terms apply to those who held office on the panel prior to 30.12.05 [reg.10(3)–(5)].

  Agencies should manage the turnover of members so as to avoid a large number of departures in any one year. Annex B also encourages a formal recruitment process for independent members [Guidance 1.16].

- The quorum for panel meetings is five including the Chair or Vice-chair, one social worker and one independent member.

- Two or more local authorities may appoint a joint panel and must agree on the Chair, Vice-chair and membership. The maximum membership for a joint panel is increased to 11 and the quorum to six [reg.3(5)].

  While there is no provision for joint panels between voluntary agencies, more than one branch of the same agency may share a panel [Guidance 1.2].

- Members may resign by giving a month's notice, or if unsuitable or unable to continue have their office terminated by the agency giving written notice with reasons (if a joint panel, all agencies must agree) [reg.4(3), (4) & (5)].

  Agencies are expected to discuss any performance shortfall with members and allow time for improvement before terminating membership [Guidance 1.24].

- The panel must take minutes of meetings including recommendations and reasons [reg.5(3)].

- Local authorities may pay reasonable fees to panel members [reg.6].

- Agencies must have agency and panel policies and procedures, drawn up in consultation with the panel, kept under review and revised as necessary [reg.7].

  Staff should also have the opportunity to contribute to policy and procedures [Guidance 1.32–3].

- Agencies must appoint a senior member of staff as agency panel adviser (by agreement if a joint panel), who must be a social worker with five years' post qualifying experience and management experience, to:

  • help with appointing, reviewing and terminating the office of panel members;

  • be responsible for training, induction and performance monitoring of panel members;

  • liaise between agency and panel and monitor panel administration [reg.8].

  When considering an intercountry adoption case the panel should have advice from a suitably experienced social worker. As the guidance also suggests a deputy panel adviser, this may be a suitable person to fulfil this role [Guidance 1.26 & 39].

  The panel adviser should also quality assure reports to panel in liaison with agency managers, and provide updates to the panel on cases previously presented [Guidance 1.40 & 41].

- Regulation 9 requires agencies to appoint at least one medical adviser and to consult her/him on dealing with medical information under the regulations.

Members should be given performance targets and reviewed against these every year. The Chair's performance is to be reviewed by the agency's decision maker. Councillors and management members are to be appointed on the same basis as all other members [Guidance 1.17–19].

Considering adoption for a child

- Regulations 12–17 cover agency duties when considering adoption for a child.

- Agencies must first create a 'child's case record' containing the prescribed information, including the 'child's permanence report' [reg.12(1)].

- If reasonably practicable (unless satisfied it has been done by another agency) the agency must:

  - counsel the child;

  - explain and provide information in writing about the process and legal implications of adoption, in an age-appropriate way;

  - ascertain the child's wishes and feelings about adoption, placement, religion and culture, and contact with parents/guardians, relatives and relevant others [reg.13].

  Guidance 2.13–16 covers counselling and informing children.

- If reasonably practicable (unless satisfied it has been done by another agency) the agency must:

  - counsel the child's parent or guardian;

  - explain and provide written information to them about adoption and placement procedures, the legal implications of giving consent to placement or future adoption, placement orders, and adoption;

  - ascertain the wishes and feelings of the child's parent/guardian and any relevant others about the child, adoption and placement for adoption, religion and culture and contact [reg.14(1) & (2)].

■ If the agency knows the identity of a father without parental responsibility, it must, if appropriate (unless satisfied it has been done by another agency):

   • counsel him;

   • explain and provide written information about adoption and placement procedures and the legal implications of adoption;

   • ascertain his wishes and feelings about the child, adoption and placement for adoption, religion and culture and contact [reg.14(3) & (4)(a)].

■ As far as possible the agency must also ascertain if a known father without parental responsibility wishes to acquire it, or to apply for a contact order [reg.14(4)(b)].

   See Guidance 2.24–25 on counselling parents about contact and providing independent advice and support; 2.27–29 on parents who refuse counselling; and 2.32–33 on obtaining information about the child.

■ Regulation 15(1) requires agencies to collect as far as possible the information about a child specified in Schedule 1 Part 1.

■ Unless a child capable of making an informed decision refuses, the agency must arrange a medical examination and obtain a 'child's health report' covering:

   • her/his state of health;

   • any treatment she/he is receiving or health care needed; and

   • the information specified in Schedule 1 Part 2 [reg.15(2), (3) & (4)].

   A medical examination may not be necessary if the medical adviser is satisfied with the information available from recent reports [Guidance 2.44].

- As far as reasonably practicable, agencies must obtain:

  - information about the child's family specified in Schedule 1 Part 3; and

  - information about the health of the child's parents and siblings specified in Schedule 1 Part 4 [reg.16].

- Agencies must prepare a 'child's permanence report' containing:

  - information specified in Schedule 1 Parts 1 and 3 (child and family);

  - medical adviser's health summary;

  - child's wishes and feelings [reg.13(1)(c)];

  - wishes and feelings of parents/guardians, father without parental responsibility (if consulted under regulation 14) and any relevant others [reg.14(1)(c)];

  - the agency's views and proposals as to contact;

  - a developmental assessment and any needs arising;

  - an assessment of the parenting capacity of parents, guardians or father without parental responsibility (if consulted under regulation 14);

  - chronology of agency decisions and actions;

  - care options considered and reason for adoption recommendation; and

  - any other relevant information [reg.17(1)].

  Parents (and child if old enough) should see part or all of the report and any views they express should be reported to the panel [Guidance 2.51 & 53].

- Agencies must send to the panel the child's permanence report, health report and any other information collected under regulations 15 and 16(2), and, as far as practicable, any other information requested by the panel [reg.17(2) & (3)].

■ The panel must consider all children referred by the agency and recommend whether the child should be placed for adoption [reg.18(1)].

■ The panel must have regard to the following requirements of section 1 of the Act:

  • section 1(2) (paramountcy);

  • section 1(4) (welfare checklist);

  • section 1(5) (race, religion, culture and language); and

  • section 1(6) (no/lesser order principle) [reg.18(2)].

■ The panel must consider the reports and information sent by the agency and must take legal advice. It may ask for more information [reg.18(2)(a)–(c)].

■ If recommending adoption, the panel must consider, and may advise on, contact and a placement order application [reg.18(3)].

■ The agency decision must take account of the panel's recommendation, and panel members must take no part in it [reg.19(1) & (2)].

  If the agency decision maker is minded not to agree the panel's recommendation, she/he should discuss this with another senior person in the agency who is not a panel member [Guidance 2.60].

■ If their whereabouts are known, the agency must notify in writing the child's parents or guardians and father without parental responsibility (if consulted under regulation 14) [reg.19(3)].

Timescales to be adhered to, unless inconsistent with the child's welfare, are set out in Guidance 2.1.

- Regulation 20 requires agencies to request the appointment of a CAFCASS officer or a Welsh Family Proceedings Officer to witness consent to placement or future adoption under sections 19 or 20 of the Act, and to send the information specified in Schedule 2.

- Any notice on file under section 20(4) (not wishing to be informed of adoption application or withdrawing such) must be sent to the court when the agency is notified of an adoption application [reg.12(2)].

Advice on the procedure to be followed in cases where a relinquished child is under six weeks old is found in Annex B of the statutory guidance, paragraphs 25–32.

Guidance Annex B paragraphs 12–22 also contains useful advice on cases where a mother refuses to disclose the identity of the father.

Approving adopters
- Unless satisfied that another agency has done so, agencies considering prospective adopters must:

  - counsel them, and

  - explain and provide written information about the procedures for and legal implications of adoption and placement for adoption (with specific reference to the proposed country in an intercountry adoption case) [reg.21].

- On receipt of a written application from a prospective adopter they have counselled under regulation 21, agencies must consider their suitability, and must set up a file ('the prospective adopter's case record') containing:

  - the application;

- information and reports obtained under regulations 22–30;

- the prospective adopter's report and their comments on it;

- panel minutes including recommendation, reasons and any advice;

- the agency decision and notifications;

- any independent review Panel recommendation;

- any prospective adopter's review report and their comments on it;

- any other relevant documents or information [reg.22(1) & (3)].

■ Agencies may ask prospective adopters for any other reasonable information in writing [reg.22(2)].

■ Agencies must seek enhanced Criminal Record Bureau (CRB) certificates for prospective adopters and members of their household aged 18 or over [reg.23(1)].

■ Agencies may not consider as a prospective adopter anyone where she/he or a member of the household aged 18 or over has been convicted of or cautioned for any offence listed in regulation 23(3) and Schedule 3 Part 1 [reg.23(2)].

■ Agencies are also precluded from considering as a prospective adopter anyone where she/he or a member of the household aged 18 or over has been convicted of or cautioned for any of the repealed offences listed in Schedule 3 Part 2 [reg.23(4)].

■ Agencies must notify the prospective adopter that she/he cannot be considered as soon as they learn that she/he or a member of the household is covered by the provisions of regulations 23(2) or (4) [reg.23(5)].

Only the person to whom the conviction relates can be told of the reason for unsuitability [Guidance 3.31].

■ Agencies must arrange preparation for prospective adopters, to cover children available for adoption, the significance of adoption for children and families, contact, the skills adopters need, adoption and placement procedures [reg.24].

Guidance 3.38 suggests that group preparation should be the standard method.

■ If the adopter appears potentially suitable, the agency must obtain the following information:

- information specified in Schedule 4 Part 1;

- written medical report after full examination, including the information specified in Schedule 4 Part 2 (unless medical adviser confirms as unnecessary);

- referee interview reports;

- written report of any relevant information from the prospective adopter's local authority [reg.25(1)–(4)].

Agencies have discretion as to whether to approach other local authorities where applicants may have lived previously [Guidance 3.45].

■ Agencies must prepare a 'prospective adopter's report' including:

- Schedule 4 Part 1 information;

- medical adviser's health summary;

- any local authority information;

- any observations on counselling, CRB checks and preparation;

- the agency's assessment of suitability to adopt; and

- any other relevant information [reg.25(5)].

■ In an intercountry adoption case, the following additional information is required:

- the proposed country of origin;

- confirmation that the prospective adopter is eligible to adopt from that country;

- any additional information required by that country; and

- the agency's assessment of the prospective adopter's suitability to adopt a child from overseas [reg.25(6)].

A "second opinion" visit by a manager or social worker should be arranged if there are concerns or issues needing clarification [Guidance 3.48].

■ Where agencies receive information suggesting that a prospective adopter is unsuitable, they may prepare the prospective adopter's report based on the information collected up to that point (a "brief report") [reg.25(7)].

■ The agency must send the prospective adopter notice of the panel and a copy of the report inviting comments on it within 10 working days [reg.25(8)].

■ After 10 working days or when comments are received, if earlier, the agency must send to the panel:

- the prospective adopter's report and their comments on it;

- the referee interview reports and any local authority information, and, if the medical adviser so advises, the medical report; and

- any other relevant information [reg.25(9)].

■ As far as is reasonably practicable, the agency must also send any other information requested by the panel [reg.25(10)].

■ The panel must consider all prospective adopters referred by the agency and recommend whether the prospective adopter is suitable to adopt a child [reg.26(1)].

- The panel must consider the reports and information sent by the agency, and may take legal advice and ask for any other necessary information [reg.26(2)].

- If the panel recommends a prospective adopter as suitable, it may also consider and advise on the number, age, sex, needs and background of children she/he should adopt [reg.26(3)].

  Agencies will be guided by such advice but are not bound by it [Guidance 3.60].

- Prospective adopters must be invited to attend the panel [reg.26(4)].

  Applicants are not obliged to attend panel and failure to attend is not an indication of unsuitability [Guidance 3.62].

- The agency must make a decision as to the prospective adopter's suitability to adopt a child and, if considered suitable, notify her/him in writing. Panel members are excluded from taking part in the decision [reg.27].

  Timescales which agencies are normally expected to meet are listed in the Guidance 3.1.

- If the agency considers the prospective adopter unsuitable, it must:

  • notify her/him in writing with reasons and the panel's recommendation, if different;

  • advise her/him of the right within 40 days of the notice to make representations to the agency or apply to the Secretary of State for an independent review [reg.27(4)].

  The form of words to be used in notifying prospective adopters that they are considered unsuitable (a 'suitability determination') is contained in Annex D of the Adoption Guidance.

- If the prospective adopter does not make representations or apply for an IRM (Independent Review Mechanism) review within 40 days, the agency should then make its decision and notify the prospective adopter in writing, with reasons [reg.27(5)].

■ If the prospective adopter does make representations, the agency may refer the case back to the panel [reg.27(6)].

■ If the agency does refer the case back, the panel must consider it and make a fresh recommendation, and the agency must make a decision based on both the original and the fresh recommendations [reg.27(7) & (8)(a)].

■ If the prospective adopter applies for an independent review, the agency must:

  • send within 10 days of receiving notice from the Secretary of State all the reports and information sent to the adoption panel, any relevant later information, and the notice with reasons (and panel recommendation if different) [reg.28];

  • make a decision after taking account of the IRM panel recommendation and the original panel recommendation [reg.27(8)(b)].

■ The agency must notify the prospective adopter in writing as soon as possible after making its decision, and:

  • if the decision is not to approve, give reasons and the panel's recommendation, where different [reg.27(9)];

  • if there was an IRM panel, send a copy of the notice to the Secretary of State [reg.27(10)].

Reviews of approved adopters
■ Agencies are required to review approved adopters unless a child has been placed or, in an intercountry case, has been linked with and visited a child overseas [reg.29(1)].

Reviews should be carried out by a manager or a social worker other than the assessor [Guidance 3.84].

- Agencies must carry out reviews at least annually, and must:

  - collect any information necessary to review the prospective adopter's suitability to adopt;

  - take account of the prospective adopter's views [reg.29(2) & (3)].

- If, on reviewing the case, the agency considers the prospective adopter no longer suitable, it must:

  - prepare a 'prospective adopter's review report' with reasons;

  - send her/him notice of the panel and a copy of the report inviting comments on it within 10 working days [reg.29(4)].

- After 10 working days or when comments are received, if earlier, the agency must send to the panel:

  - the prospective adopter's review report and their comments on it; and

  - as far as is reasonably practicable, any other information requested by the panel [reg.29(5) & (6)].

- The panel must consider the prospective adopter's review report and comments on it, any other information, and recommend whether the prospective adopter remains suitable to adopt a child [reg.29(7)].

- The agency must make a decision as to continuing suitability, and the requirements of regulation 27(2)–(10), which allow the applicant to make further representations to the agency or the IRM, apply to this decision as to the original decision [reg.29(8)].

INTERCOUNTRY ADOPTERS

- If approving a prospective adopter in intercountry cases, the agency must send the following to the Secretary of State:

- its decision and any recommendations as to the age, sex, needs and background of child they may be suitable for;

- any reports and information sent to the panel;

- the panel minute including recommendation and reasons;

- any IRM panel minute including recommendation and reasons; and

- any other relevant information [reg.30].

See Guidance 3.92–103 and Annex C for further information on the procedure in adoptions with a foreign element.

Matching a child with approved adopters

- When considering a 'proposed placement', agencies must meet the prospective adopters, counsel them and give them information (including the child's permanence report) and seek their views on the proposed placement and any contact arrangements [reg.31(1)].

- If proposing to proceed with the placement:

  - local authority agencies must assess the child and adoptive family for support needs;

  - voluntary agencies must advise the adopters that they can approach the local authority for an assessment and, if they ask, pass on reports.

- All agencies must consider contact arrangements, and prepare an 'adoption placement report' containing the prescribed information [reg.31(2)].

  Agencies may compare a number of prospective adopters for a child, but should only include details of the adopter/s finally selected in the report to panel [Guidance 4.5–6].

- The agency must give prospective adopters a copy of the report and 10 working days to comment on it, after which it will be sent to the panel (with any comments received) together with the child's permanence report and the prospective adopter's report [reg.31(3) & (4)].

- In an inter-agency case, the other agency must be consulted before the proposed placement is referred to the panel, and a child's or adopter's file (as the case may be) must be opened [reg.31(6)–(8)].

- The panel must consider any proposed placement referred by the agency and (having regard to sections 1(2), (4) & (5) of the Act) recommend whether the child should be placed with the prospective adopter [reg.32(1) & (2)].

- The panel must consider the reports sent by the agency, and may take legal advice and ask for more information [reg.32(2)(a)–(c)].

- The panel must also consider – and if approving the placement, may advise on – proposed support arrangements (local authorities), contact and any necessary restrictions on the exercise of parental responsibility [reg.32(3) & (4)].

  A detailed discussion of the considerations in relation to sharing and restricting parental responsibility is contained in the Adoption Guidance 7.30–44.

- The agency must make a decision (panel members taking no part) as to the proposed placement, having considered the panel recommendation, and as soon as possible notify in writing:

  - the adopter/s; and

  - if their whereabouts are known, the parent/guardian and if appropriate, a father without parental responsibility (if consulted under regulation 14) [reg.33(1)–(3)].

- If the agency decides the placement should proceed, it must explain this to the child in an age-appropriate way [reg.33(4)].

■ Agencies must place on the child's file:

- the prospective adopter's report;

- the adoption placement report and the adopters' comments on it;

- panel minutes with recommendations, reasons and any advice;

- decisions and notices under this regulation [reg.33(5)].

■ In intercountry cases, agencies must send the adopters any information from overseas about a child to be placed (unless they have a copy already), consider and discuss it with the adopters, and if necessary counsel them and supply any further information [reg.34].

Timescales which agencies should normally meet are set out in Guidance 4.1–3; additional guidance on intercountry cases is in 4.39 & 41–2.

■ If an agency has decided to place a child with adopters and met them to discuss arrangements, it must send them as soon as possible an 'adoption placement plan' covering the matters specified in Schedule 5 [reg.35(1) & (2)].

A draft of the placement plan should form the basis for a placement planning meeting with the adopters and others [Guidance 5.2].

■ The child may be placed once the adopters have agreed to the placement provided that the:

- agency is authorised to place the child, or

- child is under six weeks old and either the parent/guardian has consented to placement or there is a placement order [reg.35(3) & (4)].

■ If the child is already in placement, the agency must write to the adopter with the date of placement for adoption [reg.35(5)].

- Agencies must, before placement for adoption:

  - notify the adopters' GP and send health information about the child;

  - notify the local authority (if different) and the local health body; and

  - for a school age child, notify the education department and send education information [reg.35(6)].

- Agencies must notify prospective adopters of any change in placement plan [reg.35(7)].

- Agencies must place on the child's file:

  - a copy of any agreement to placement for a child under six weeks, and

  - the placement plan and any changes to it [reg.35(8)].

Reviews of children in adoption cases

- Agencies authorised to place a child for adoption who is not yet placed must review the case after three months and then every six months until placement [reg.36(1)].

- Where a child is placed for adoption, agencies must:

  - review the case within four weeks; three months after the first review; and then every six months until the child moves or is adopted; and

  - visit the child and adopter/s weekly until the first review and as necessary thereafter, and write a report of each visit; and

  - advise and assist the adopter/s as necessary [reg.36(2), (3) & (4)].

Visits should be shared between the child's and the adopters' social workers. Placing agencies may make arrangements with another local authority to visit a child placed out of the area. Children should be seen alone unless old enough to refuse [Guidance 5.16–18].

■ As far as is reasonably practicable, agencies must seek the views of the child, the adopters and any other relevant person for each review [reg.36(5)].

■ Agencies must ensure that reviews cover:

  • the continued appropriateness of placement;

  • the child's needs, welfare and development, and any necessary changes;

  • contact arrangements;

  • arrangements for exercise of parental responsibility;

  • adoption support services;

  • health and education in consultation with the relevant bodies;

  • review frequency (subject to regulation 36(1) & (3)) [reg.36(5) & (6)].

■ If a child on a placement order has not been placed for adoption by the six-months review, the agency must find out why, and consider whether any action is needed and if it is still appropriate to place the child [reg.36(7)].

■ As far as is reasonably practicable, after a review agencies must notify the child (if old enough), the adopters and any other relevant person of the outcome [reg.36(8)].

■ Agencies must record on the child's file all information obtained for a review including the child's views, the record of any meeting and of any decisions made [reg.36(9)].

■ Regulation 36(10) requires agencies to carry out a review of a child returned by the adopters between 28 and 42 days after the disruption, and consider:

  • the continued appropriateness of placement for adoption;

  • the child's needs, welfare and development, and any necessary changes;

- contact arrangements; and

- health and education in consultation with the relevant bodies.

■ Regulation 37 requires local authorities and voluntary agencies which accommodate children to appoint as an independent reviewing officer a registered social worker with sufficient experience, where 'independent' means, if an agency employee, not involved in the case or its management in any way [reg.37(1)–(4)].

■ Reviewing officers must, as far as is reasonably practicable, chair all review meetings, and ensure the requirements of regulation 36 are met, and in particular:

- the child's views are taken into account;

- people are identified to carry out decisions; and

- any failure to review or implement review decisions is reported to a senior officer [reg.37(5) & (6)].

■ Reviewing officers must assist a child who wishes to bring court proceedings to obtain legal advice or identify an appropriate adult to assist or act on the child's behalf [reg.37(7)].

■ Agencies must notify the independent reviewing officer (IRO) of any change in circumstances or any failure to implement review decisions [reg.37(8)].

■ Regulation 38 provides for what happens if a parent withdraws consent given under section 19 or 20 of the Act [reg.38(1)]. In this event:

- voluntary agencies must immediately consider whether to inform the local authority where the child is [reg.38(3)];

- local authorities must immediately review the decision to place for adoption and, if they decide to apply for a placement order, notify as soon as possible the parent or guardian, a father without parental responsibility (if consulted under regulation 14) and the adopters if the child is already placed [reg.38(2)].

Records

■ Agencies must ensure that children's and adopters' records are kept securely and confidentially, and are protected from theft, unauthorised disclosure, damage or destruction, for as long as necessary [regs.39–41].

Agencies must have systems in place to protect electronically stored records [Guidance 6.4].

■ Agencies must allow access to records and disclose information as required and must record any such disclosure [reg.42].

Regulations 40–42 do not apply to section 56 information [reg.44] – see also Disclosure of Adoption Information (Post-Commencement Adoptions) Regulations 2005.

■ Agencies may transfer children's or adopters' records to other agencies where appropriate but must record all such transfers [reg.43(1)].

■ Regulation 43 provides for transfer of records to another agency.

Child under six weeks of age

■ Regulation 45 clarifies the application of parts of the Children Act 1989 in cases where an agency is authorised to place a child or a child under six weeks is placed for adoption.

The effect of this regulation is clarified in the statutory guidance. In summary, it removes the duty to consult parents and substitutes consultation with the adopters; it also removes the duty to promote contact and the parents' obligation to contribute to the child's maintenance [Guidance 7.1–4, 19–21 & Annex B].

Contact

- If an agency decides to place a child for adoption, it must consider and decide upon contact arrangements, taking into account:

  - the views of the parent/guardian, and father without parental responsibility if consulted under regulation 14;

  - any panel advice;

  - the considerations of section 1(2) & (4) of the Act [reg.46(1)–(3)].

- Agencies must notify contact arrangements to, and if proposing any change, seek and take account of the views of:

  - the child (if old enough);

  - if their whereabouts are known, the parent/guardian and, if appropriate, a father without parental responsibility (if consulted under regulation 14);

  - anyone who previously had contact under the 1989 Act; and

  - any other relevant person [reg.46(4) & (6)].

- Agencies must review contact arrangements after deciding to place a child in the light of the prospective adopters' views and any advice given by the panel [reg.46(5)].

- Agencies must set out contact arrangements in the placement plan and keep reviewing them [reg.46(7)].

- Regulation 47 provides for variation of contact under a section 26 order.

- Contact may be varied by agreement with the person having contact, subject to the child's agreement (if old enough) and that of the adopters (if child placed for adoption), and after confirmation is sent to all three [reg.47(2) & (3)].

■ Contact may be refused under section 27(2) provided the child (if old enough), the person having contact and the adopters (if child placed) are notified immediately of the decision, date taken, reasons for and duration of refusal [reg.47(1) & (3)].

Adoption Support Services Regulations 2005

These regulations apply to England only and provide for local authority adoption support services.

■ Regulation 2 sets out definitions of terms, in particular:

- 'adoptive child' means
  - a child who has been adopted or in respect of whom notice of intention to be adopted has been given, or
  - a child matched with prospective adopters or placed for adoption by an adoption agency and includes, for the purposes of financial support, an adopted person over the age of 18 continuing in full-time education [reg.2(1)1 and (2)2];

- 'adoptive parent' means a person who has adopted, or given notice of intention to adopt, or been matched with, or had placed for adoption, a child;

- 'agency adoptive child' means a child who has been adopted after an agency placement, matched or placed with adopters by an agency, or whose adoptive parent was a local authority foster carer (unless the authority opposed the adoption);

- the definition of 'related to' an adoptive child includes anyone where the relationship is judged to be beneficial to her/his welfare, taking account of the welfare checklist [reg.2(1)];

■ The services to be provided are:

- counselling, advice and information [s.2(6)(b) of the Act];

- financial support;

- support groups for adopters, adopted children and their birth parents/former guardians;

- assistance with contact – including mediation – between adopted children and their natural parents or relatives (includes siblings), and with others where the relationship is judged to be beneficial to the child's welfare;

- therapeutic services to adoptive children;

- services to maintain an adoption including training for adopters to meet a child's special needs and respite care (subject to the requirements on accommodating children under sections 23 or 59 Children Act 1989);

- assistance with or to prevent a disruption, including mediation and disruption meetings [reg.3(1)].

■ Regulation 3(2) excludes provision of the above services for adoptions by parents, step-parents and parents' partners.

■ Group support, contact assistance, therapy and services to maintain adoptions may be provided by making payments [reg.3(3)].

■ Regulation 4 sets out the entitlement of certain people to prescribed services.

■ The following are entitled to counselling, advice and information:

- children and their parents/guardians;

- prospective adopters;

- adoptees and their parents, birth parents/former guardians;

- adopters' children;

- those related to adoptive children (see definition under regulation 2(2) above) including birth siblings [reg.3(2)].

■ Adopters of agency adoptive children are eligible for financial support [reg.3(3)].

■ Support groups must be made available to agency adoptive children and their adopters, birth parents/former guardians [reg.3(4)].

■ Contact support must be made available to agency adoptive children and their adopters, birth parents/former guardians and birth siblings [reg.3(5)].

■ Therapeutic services must be made available to agency adoptive children and those adopted from abroad [reg.3(6)].

■ Disruption support must be made available to agency adoptive children, those adopted from abroad, their adopters and any children of the adopters [reg.3(7)].

■ Under regulation 5, support services may be contracted out to:

- local authorities;

- adoption support agencies;

- PCTs (Health Boards);

- education departments.

- but under the Act, they can also be contracted out to voluntary adoption agencies.

Adoption Support Services Adviser (ASSA)

■ Local authorities must appoint an 'adoption support services adviser' (ASSA) with sufficient knowledge and experience of adoption and its effect, to give advice and information about services to anyone affected by adoption [reg.6(1), (2)(a) and (3)].

- The ASSA will also advise the local authority on adoption support assessments, services and plans, and liaise with other local authorities [reg.6(2)(b)].

  Advice on the appointment and role of the ASSA will be found in the Guidance (9.9–19).

Responsibility for support outside local authority area

- Under section 4 of the Act, local authorities are responsible for adoption support to children they have placed outside their area, their adopters and any children of those adopters until three years after the adoption order; however, the responsibility for ongoing financial support continues as long as eligibility [reg.7(1) and (2)].

- Authorities have discretion to provide support to others outside their area as appropriate [reg.7(3)].

Financial support

- Regulation 8 provides that financial support to maintain an adoptive placement/adoption may only be paid to adopters where:

  - it is necessary to ensure the child can be looked after;

  - greater resources are required because of illness, disability, emotional or behavioural difficulties or the effects of abuse or neglect;

  - special arrangements are necessary because of age or ethnic origin or to enable a child to be placed with a sibling or another child she/he has lived with;

  - it is to meet regular travel costs for contact;

  - as a contribution to adoption legal costs (including court fees), introductions or setting up costs, including:

    - furniture and equipment;

    - adaptations to the home;

- transport;

- clothing, toys or other necessary items.

Local authorities are not required to pay legal costs for non-agency adoptions or those they oppose [Guidance 9.57].

■ Financial support may only include a reward element:

  • where the adopter was the child's foster carer, and

  • the fostering allowance included a reward element [reg.9(1)].

■ The reward element is payable for two years from adoption (longer in exceptional circumstances at the local authority's discretion) [reg.9(2)].

■ Financial support is to be by way of a single payment except:

  • to meet a recurring need, in which case a periodic payment (i.e. regular allowance) may be paid;

  • by agreement, in instalments [reg.10].

■ Financial support stops when the child:

  • no longer has a home with the adopter(s);

  • leaves full-time education and either starts work or qualifies for income support or jobseeker's allowance;

  • reaches 18, unless continuing in full-time education, when it may continue until the end of that course [reg.11].

■ In order to receive periodic payments of financial support, adopters (both if a couple) must agree to:

  • notify the local authority immediately (and if orally, confirm in writing in seven days) of any new address, the child's death, any changes listed in regulation 11 and any change in financial circumstances or the financial needs or resources of the child;

- supply an annual statement of financial circumstances and the financial needs and resources of the child, plus confirmation of address and that the child is still there [reg.12(1)].

■ Local authorities may impose conditions on payments, including how and when they are to be spent [reg.12(2)].

■ Payments may be suspended or stopped if any conditions are not met, and the local authority may seek repayment of part or all of the amount paid; however, in the case of failure to supply an annual statement, the authority must first send a reminder giving 28 days to comply [reg.12(3) & (4)].

■ A notice must be sent to the adopters (see under Regulation 18(3) below).

Financial support should be calculated by reference to the fostering allowance which would be payable for the particular child [Guidance 9.52].

Assessment for adoption support
■ Local authorities must assess support needs (s.4(1)(b) of the Act) at the request of:

- adopters' children;

- those related to adoptive children (see definition under Regulation 2(2) above) including birth siblings [reg.13(1)].

- in addition to those entitled to assessment under the Act [s.3(1)].

■ The assessment may be carried out just in relation to a particular service if the person requests it or the authority so decides [reg.13(2)].

■ Local authorities do not have to assess the need of people for a particular support service if they are not listed as eligible for that service in regulation 4 [reg.13(4)].

■ Assessments must consider any of the following which are relevant:

  • the person's needs and how they might be met;

  • the adoptive family's needs and how they might be met;

  • child's developmental and other needs and how they might be met;

  • the adopter's parenting capacity;

  • family and environment;

  • circumstances leading to placement for adoption;

  • any previous assessments of the person's support needs [reg.14(1)].

■ The local authority must, if appropriate, interview the subject of any
   assessment, and if a child, also interview the adopter(s) [reg.14(3)].

■ If health or education services appear to be needed, the relevant body
   must be consulted as part of the assessment [reg.14(4)].

■ Local authorities must write a report of the assessment [reg.14(3)].

■ In deciding an amount of financial support, local authorities must take
   account of any grant, benefit, allowance or resource available to the person
   as an adopter [reg.15(2)].

■ Unless regulation 15(4) or (5) applies, local authorities must also take
   account of:

  • the person's financial resources, including state benefits payable for the
    child;

  • the person's reasonable outgoings and commitments (excluding the child);

  • the child's financial needs and resources [reg.15(3)].

■ Under regulation 15(4) local authorities must disregard the means test in regulation 15(3) if paying legal costs to support an application to adopt an agency child.

■ Regulation 15(5) allows local authorities to disregard the regulation 15(3) means test when paying:

- setting-up or special care costs for an agency child;

- ongoing travel costs for contact purposes;

- any reward element under regulation 9 (former foster carer).

■ Except for advice and information or one-off support, local authorities must draw up a support services plan [reg.16(2)].

■ If health or education services appear to be needed, the relevant body must be consulted before the drawing up of the plan [reg.16(3)].

■ Local authorities must nominate someone to monitor the plan's implementation [reg.16(4)].

■ People must be given the chance to make representations before a decision about support needs is made, having first been notified of the proposed decision and the time allowed for making representations [reg.17(1) & (2)].

■ The notice must state:

- the person's support needs;

- the basis for determining any financial support and the amount payable;

- if the local authority proposes to provide any support services, and if so which services;

- any conditions to be imposed [reg.17(3)].

■ If services are to be provided and a plan is required, a draft plan must accompany the notice [reg.17(4)].

■ No decision can be made until:

- the person has made representations or accepted the proposal and any draft plan, or

- the time limit has expired [reg.17(5)].

■ When the local authority has made a decision about providing support services, it must notify the person, with reasons [reg.18(1)].

■ If a plan is required, the notice must include the plan and the person nominated to monitor it [reg.18(2)].

■ For financial support, the notice must state:

- how the amount is calculated;

- the amount, frequency, period and start date of payments by instalments;

- the date of any one-off payment;

- any conditions attached, any date by which they are to be met and what happens if they are not met;

- review, variation and termination procedures;

- the local authority's and adopter's respective responsibilities with regard to payment and reviews [reg.18(3)].

Reviews of adoption support

■ Reviews of periodic financial support are covered by regulation 20 and of other services by regulation 19.

■ Regulation 19(2) requires the local authority to review provision at least annually, and if the person's circumstances change, and at any other time appropriate to the plan.

- Reviews must be conducted as for assessments in accordance with regulations 14 and 15 [reg.19(3)].

- People must be given the chance to make representations before a decision about variation or termination of support services is made, having first been notified of the proposed decision and the time allowed for making representations. The notice must contain the information listed in regulation 17(3) and any revised draft plan [reg.19(4) & (5)].

- Local authorities must make a decision about variation or termination based on the review and any representations, and if necessary revise the plan; they must then notify the person, with reasons and details of any revised plan [reg.19(6) & (7)].

- Regulation 20(2) requires local authorities to review financial support on receipt of the annual statement, and if the person's circumstances change or any condition is breached, and at any other time appropriate to the plan.

- Reviews must be conducted as for assessments in accordance with regulations 14 and 15 [reg.20(4)].

- People must be given the chance to make representations before a decision to reduce or stop payments or revise the plan, having first been notified of the proposed decision and the time allowed for making representations. The notice must contain the information listed in regulation 17(3) and any revised draft plan [reg.20(5) & (7)].

- Payments may be suspended pending a decision [reg.20(6)].

- Local authorities must make a decision about variation, termination or recovery of any payments made, based on the review and any representations, and if necessary revise the plan; they must then notify the person, with reasons and details of any revised plan [reg.20(8) & (9)].

The form the review takes will vary according to the service, from correspondence only to a full reassessment [Guidance 9.76–7].

- In urgent cases, the local authority may disregard any requirement to assess, plan or notify which would delay service provision [reg.21].

- Regulation 22 requires notices to be in writing, and in the case of a child who is not of sufficient age or understanding or where the local authority deems it inappropriate, to be given to the adopter or other appropriate adult.

- Regulation 23 enables area local authorities providing support services (except advice and information) to recover their costs from placing local authorities unless that authority is required to provide services under regulation 7.

- Assessments, plans, reviews and support services under the 2003 Regulations on 30.12.05 are treated as effective under these Regulations.

Independent Review of Determinations (Adoption) Regulations 2005

- These regulations apply to England only and implement section 12 of the Act. They cover two types of adoption agency decisions:

  - not to approve a prospective adopter under the Adoption Agencies Regulations 2005 (a 'suitability determination');

  - about disclosure or non-disclosure of information in accordance with the Disclosure of Adoption Information (Post-Commencement Adoptions) Regulations 2005 (a 'disclosure determination') [reg.1–3].

Guidance on the use of the Independent Review Mechanism (IRM) for suitability determinations is found in Annex D of the Adoption Guidance.

- Regulation 4 provides for the setting up of panels to review applications received by the Secretary of State [reg.4(1)]. Membership of the panel is drawn from a list maintained by the Secretary of State [reg.4(2)] to include social workers (with three years' post-qualifying child care experience, including adoption), registered medical practitioners and others including, where practicable, people with personal experience of adoption [reg.4(3)].

- Panels reviewing a suitability determination will have a maximum of 10 members including at least two social workers, a medical adviser and four other members, including two with personal experience of adoption where practicable [reg.4(4)].

- Panels reviewing a disclosure determination consist of three members including two social workers [reg.4(5)].

- The Secretary of State appoints a suitably experienced Chair, and for a suitability case, one of the members as Vice-chair [reg.4(6)].

- The following are prohibited from being on the panel:

  - any member of the panel which made the decision being reviewed;

  - employees of the agency within two years of the decision;

  - elected members of a local authority agency or those involved in the management of a voluntary agency within two years of the decision;

  - anyone related to one of the above;

  - adopters approved by or of a child placed by the agency;

  - anyone adopted through the agency;

  - anyone with personal or professional knowledge of the applicant [reg.4(7)].

- Regulation 4(8) defines 'employed' as paid or voluntary and 'related to' as including married to or civil partner of a person, household member, child, parent or sibling of the person or married to/civil partner of that person.

- Regulation 5 provides for panels reviewing a suitability case.

- The panel must take account of all information provided, may request other information or assistance from the agency and may take legal advice [reg.5(5)].

- The panel must review the decision and make a recommendation to the agency. The recommendation can be that:

  - the adopter is suitable to adopt a child (if the prospective adopter's report complied with regulation 25, Adoption Agencies Regulations);

  - the agency should prepare a report which complies with regulation 25, Adoption Agencies Regulations;

  - the adopter is not suitable to adopt a child [reg.5(2)–(4)].

- Regulation 6 provides for panels reviewing a disclosure case.

- The panel must review the decision and recommend whether or not the agency should proceed with its original decision [reg.6(2)].

- The panel must take account of all information provided, may request other information or assistance from the agency and may take legal advice [reg.6(3)].

- Panels members may be paid expenses [reg.7].

- The quorum for a suitability panel meeting is five, including the Chair or Vice-chair and a social worker [reg.8(1)].

- For a disclosure panel, all three members must be present [reg.8(2)].

- Records are to be kept securely for 12 months and must include the reasons for the recommendation and whether it was a unanimous or majority recommendation [reg.9].

- An application for a panel review must be in writing and state the grounds for applying [reg.10].

- The application will be acknowledged and a copy sent to the agency. A panel will be set up and the applicant will be notified of the arrangements. Applicants have until two weeks before the meeting to provide further written details and may also address the panel [reg.11].

- The panel's recommendation may be a majority decision [reg.12(1)].

- The panel record must give reasons for the recommendation, state whether it is unanimous or by a majority, be signed and dated by the Chair and be sent to the applicant and the agency without delay [reg.12(2) & (3)].

- The panel may order the agency to pay reasonable costs [reg.13].

Adoptions with a Foreign Element Regulations 2005

- These regulations apply to England and Wales and make provision relating to adoptions with a foreign element under the Adoption (Intercountry Aspects) Act 1999 and the 2002 Act. They supplement and should be read in conjunction with the Adoption Agencies Regulations 2005.

  Further information on adoptions with a foreign element, including very helpful flowcharts showing the procedure to be followed in, and tables setting out the immigration requirements for, different types of adoption, is to be found in Annex C of the Adoption Guidance.

Bringing a child into the UK
- Regulation 3 requires anyone who intends to bring a child into the UK for adoption (or adopted overseas in the last six months) to apply in writing for assessment by an adoption agency and to supply any information required for the assessment.

- Before bringing a child into the UK, a prospective adopter must have received a notice from the Secretary of State that a certificate has been issued to the overseas authority confirming:

  - their approval and eligibility to adopt, and

  - that a child if adopted and granted entry clearance will have permanent right of residence in the UK [reg.4(2)(a)].

- The prospective adopter/s must visit a child in the country of origin before bringing her/him into the UK [reg.4(2)(c)] and afterwards:

  - confirm the visit and intention to proceed, in writing, to the agency;

  - provide any additional reports or information;

  - notify the agency of the expected date when the child will be brought to the UK [reg.4(2)(d)].

- Before visiting the child overseas, a prospective adopter must:

  - provide the adoption agency with any reports and information received about the child;

  - meet the agency to discuss the proposed match [reg.4(2)(b)].

- Regulation 4(3) requires the adopter/s to accompany the child to the UK unless the agency and the overseas authority agree that only one of a couple needs to do so.

- Unless the child is adopted or to be adopted overseas, the prospective adopter must notify their local authority within 14 days of:

  - the child's arrival in the UK, and

  - her/his intention to apply to adopt (or not to keep the child) [reg.4(4)].

- If the prospective adopter subsequently moves to a new area, she/he must notify the new local authority within 14 days [reg.4(5)].

■ Once notified, the local authority must:

- set up a file containing information from the overseas authority, adoption agency, prospective adopter, entry clearance officer and Secretary of State/Welsh Assembly [reg.5(1)(a)];

- notify the prospective adopter's GP and PCT/Local Health Board and send any health information to the GP [reg.5(1)(b) & (c)];

- notify the education department if the child is of school age, and send any educational information, including the likelihood of an assessment of special educational needs [reg.5(1)(d)];

- visit the child and the prospective adopter within one week; then at least weekly until the first review; and at its discretion thereafter until the child moves or is adopted; and in each visit advise on adoption support services as necessary [reg.5(1)(e) & (h)(iii)];

- review the case within four weeks of the notice, three months after the first review if necessary and at six-monthly intervals thereafter until the child moves or is adopted [reg.5(1)(f)];

- advise on the child's needs, welfare and development [reg.5(1)(h)(i)].

■ Reviews must consider the child's needs, welfare and development and any changes required; adoption support and if reassessment is needed; and the need for further reviews [reg.5(1)(g)].

■ Written reports of all visits and reviews must be placed on the child's file [reg.5(1)(h)(ii)].

■ Files must comply with Part 7 of the Adoption Agencies Regulations or the Welsh equivalent [reg.5(2)].

■ The local authority must review the case if no application is made within two years, and consider:

- the child's needs, welfare and development and any necessary changes;

- the exercise of parental responsibility;

- entry terms and immigration status;

- adoption support and if a reassessment is needed;

- with other agencies, health and education needs [reg.5(3) & (4)].

■ If notified that a prospective adopter will move or has moved to another local authority area, a local authority must notify the new authority within 14 days and send full details, including the date of the original notice of intention to adopt [reg.5(5)].

■ Regulations 6–9 clarify the application of Chapter 3 of the 2002 Act to intercountry adoption cases in relation to removal [reg.6]; change of name and removal from the UK [reg.7]; return of the child [reg.8]; and period of time the child must live with the adopter/s before an application is made which is:

- six months if requirements have been met, or

- 12 months if not [reg.9].

■ Regulation 10 sets out the conditions to be met in cases where a parental responsibility order is sought to enable a child to be taken abroad for adoption (s.84 of the Act).

■ Regulation 11 extends certain provisions of the Act relating to adoption orders to section 84 orders.

Hague Convention adoptions – British applicants
■ Regulations 12–34 inclusive apply to Hague Convention adoptions of children from overseas by British applicants.

■ Prospective adopters must:

- be 21 or over;

- have been habitually resident in the UK for not less than a year;

- apply in writing to an agency for an assessment;

- give any information required for the assessment [reg.13].

■ Unless satisfied that another agency has done so, agencies must counsel applicants in accordance with regulation 21 Adoption Agencies Regulations and also give them verbal and written information about adopting from their chosen country [reg.14].

■ The requirements of regulations 22–26 Adoption Agencies Regulations apply in relation to checks, preparation, assessment, approval and record-keeping. The prospective adopter's report must cover:

- proposed state of origin;

- eligibility to adopt from that country;

- information required for that country; and

- suitability to adopt from that country [reg.15].

■ The agency must make a decision in accordance with regulation 27 Adoption Agencies Regulations [reg.16].

■ Approval must be reviewed annually until a child is matched under regulation 29 Adoption Agencies Regulations [reg.17].

■ In Hague Convention cases, all documentation must be sent by the agency to the UK Central Authority, which will pass it on to the Central Authority in the state of origin, and write to the agency and the adopter confirming that this has been done [reg.18].

■ The overseas Central Authority will send information about a matched child to the UK Central Authority, which must pass it on to the agency [reg.19(1)].

- The agency must consider the proposed match, send the information to the adopter/s and meet them to discuss it and appropriate support, and if necessary counsel them [reg.19(2)].

- The adopters (both if a couple) must visit the child, provide any further information to the agency and then write to confirm an intention to proceed with adoption; the agency must notify the UK Central Authority in writing that this has been done and that it is in agreement [reg.19(3)].

- The UK Central Authority then notifies the overseas Central Authority of the adopter's wish to proceed and its agreement, and confirms authority for the child to enter and live in the UK [reg.19(4)].

- The adopters and the agency must be informed when the two Central Authorities have reached agreement [reg.19(5)].

- If the overseas Central Authority decides not to proceed with the match, the UK Central Authority informs the agency which informs the adopters; if the agency reviews the adopter/s and decides they are no longer suitable, or if the adopters withdraw, the agency informs the UK Central Authority which informs the overseas Central Authority; in all cases the information on the child must be returned to the overseas Central Authority [reg.20].

- The adopter/s must notify the agency when they propose to bring the child into the UK, confirm when the child is placed and accompany the child to the UK (both adopters unless the agency and the overseas Central Authority agree that only one of a couple needs to do so) [reg.21].

- Before the child enters the UK, the agency must notify the prospective adopter's GP and PCT/Local Health Board and send any health information to the GP; notify the local authority (if not the agency); and notify the education department if the child is of school age, and send any educational information, including the likelihood of an assessment of special educational needs [reg.22].

- If a child is brought to the UK in a Hague Convention case without first being adopted abroad, the prospective adopter must notify their local authority within 14 days of the child's arrival in the UK, and her/his intention to apply to adopt (or not to keep the child), and if she/he moves, must also notify the new local authority within 14 days of moving [reg.24].

- A local authority notified under regulation 24 must comply with the requirements of regulation 5 as for non-Convention cases [reg.25].

- If the adopter notifies a local authority that she/he does not wish to proceed with the adoption, the child must be returned within seven days and the local authority must notify the UK Central Authority [reg.26].

- If a local authority decides the placement is not in the child's best interests, it must notify the adopters and the UK Central Authority; the adopters must return the child within seven days, subject to any order of a Court where an adoption application is pending [reg.27].

- Regulation 28 requires local authorities to arrange new adoptive placements for children who are returned or removed, or where a Convention adoption order is refused or annulled (provided the local authority is satisfied it is in the child's best interests). If the local authority is not satisfied that another UK placement is in the child's best interests, it must liaise with the UK Central Authority to arrange her/his return to the country of origin. In either case, the local authority must consider the child's wishes and feelings (subject to age and understanding) and obtain her/his consent if appropriate.

- Local authorities must comply with any request for a report in cases where a child is brought to the UK under a Convention adoption order which is subject to a probationary period, and the report must contain the requested information and be submitted on time [reg.29].

- Regulation 30 specifies additional information for Hague Convention cases to be included in a Court report under section 44(5) of the Act.

- Regulation 31 sets out the requirements for the making of a Convention adoption order:

  - the applicant, or both applicants if a couple, must have been habitually resident in the UK for at least a year;

  - the child was previously resident in a Convention country overseas; and

  - if neither of the applicants is a British citizen, the child has been authorised to enter and live in the UK.

- The UK Central Authority must issue a Schedule 2 certificate when a Convention adoption order is made in England or Wales and send it to the overseas Central Authority, the adopter/s, the agency and (if different) the local authority [reg.32(1)].

- When a Convention adoption order is made overseas, the UK Central Authority will receive a certificate and must send a copy to the adopter/s, the agency and (if different) the local authority [reg.32(2)].

- If a Convention adoption application is withdrawn or refused, the adopter must return the child to the local authority when directed by the Court [reg.33].

- An order annulling a Convention adoption will be sent to the UK Central Authority which must send a copy to the overseas Central Authority [reg.34].

Hague Convention adoptions – overseas applicants
- Regulations 35–51 inclusive apply to Hague Convention adoptions of British children by overseas adopters.

- Unless satisfied that another agency has done so, an agency must in Convention cases comply with the requirements of regulations 13 (counselling and information for the child) and 14 (counselling and information for the parents) Adoption Agencies Regulations, including additional information about Convention adoption [regs.36 & 37].

- The child's permanence report (reg.17, Adoption Agencies Regulations) must include assessment of whether a child could be adopted in the UK and if adoption overseas is in her/his best interests. The report must be sent to the panel together with any reports received from overseas and the agency's comments on them, and the panel must consider these [regs.38 & 39].

- Agencies which make a decision to place a child for a Convention adoption must send full details to the UK Central Authority (which will keep a list) and notify the Central Authority if the child is placed in the UK or the best interest decision is changed [regs.40 & 41].

- UK Central Authorities will match children on the list with prospective adopters in overseas Convention countries who meets the requirements (unless the adopter has been identified for a named child) and notify the referring local authority [reg.42].

- The agency and panel must consider whether the proposed placement should proceed, and the panel must consider any reports and information sent [regs.43 & 44].

- The requirements of regulation 33(3) Adoption Agencies Regulations to notify the adopters and the child's parents of its decision do not apply, but the agency must notify the UK Central Authority as soon as possible, and if not agreeing to the placement, return all documents to the UK Central Authority for return to the overseas Central Authority [reg.45].

- If agreeing to the placement, the agency must prepare a report covering the information required by Schedule 1 Adoption Agencies Regulations (in effect, a child's permanence report) and send it, together with details of any court orders and confirmation of parental consent, to the UK Central Authority to be passed to the overseas Central Authority [reg.46].

- The UK Central Authority can agree to the proposed placement provided that:

- the adopters have agreed to proceed, have visited the child and have agreed to travel with the child;

- adopters in Convention cases have been advised to apply for a parental responsibility order [s.84(1) of the Act];

- the child will have the right of entry and residence in the receiving state [reg.47(1)–(2) & (4)].

■ Agencies may not place the child until advised by the UK Central Authority that agreement has been reached [reg.47(3)].

Conditions for a parental responsibility order under section 84

■ The relevant overseas bodies must prepare a report on the adopters, confirm their eligibility, counsel them and confirm the child's eligibility to enter and live in the receiving state.

■ The UK agency must prepare a report on the child; comply with the Adoption Agencies Regulations and these Regulations; supply the Court with the child's permanence report, the panel's recommendations and the adoption placement report; include in its court report (sections 43(a) and 44(5) of the Act) details of any visits and reviews, and in a Convention case, copies of the required Convention reports and agreement.

■ The adopters have agreed in writing to travel with the child (unless agreed that only one of a couple need do so) [reg.48 & 49].

Convention adoption orders

■ Convention adoption orders can only be made if:

- the adopters (both if a couple) have been habitually resident in the receiving state for no less than a year;

- the child was resident in the UK when the agreement was made;

- the child's right to enter and remain in the receiving state has been confirmed [reg.50].

- When a UK Central Authority receives a Convention adoption order, it must issue a Schedule 2 Certificate and send it to the overseas Central Authority and the local authority; and if it receives a certificate issued by another UK Central Authority, it must send that to the local authority [reg.51].

- Regulation 52 provides that the Act (as modified in the succeeding regulations) applies to Convention adoptions unless clearly contradictory.

- Regulations 53–58 make minor modifications to certain sections of the Act for the purpose of Convention adoptions.

- Regulation 59 makes it an offence to fail to notify the local authority under Regulation 24 or comply with a requirement to return a child under regulations 26, 27 or 33.

Adopted Children and Adoption Contact Registers Regulations 2005

- These regulations apply to England and Wales and govern the operation of the Adopted Children Register and the Adoption Contact Register.

- Regulation 2 prescribes the form for entries in the Adopted Children Register as set out in Schedule 1 (England) and Schedule 2 (Wales).

- Under regulation 3, foreign adoptions are registrable if the adopter (or both adopters if a couple) is habitually resident in England or Wales.

- Regulation 4 provides that an application to register a child adopted under a registrable foreign adoption may be made by:

  - the adopters (or one of them);

- anyone with parental responsibility;

- the adopted person if over 18.

■ An application must be in writing and accompanied by prescribed documents and other information [reg.5(1) & (2)].

■ Applicants must arrange for documents which are not in English or Welsh to be translated into English (sic) [reg.5(4)].

■ Regulation 6 prescribes the information to be held in Part 1 of the Adoption Contact Register (and Schedule 3 the form):

- adoptee's name, address and date of birth, and

- relatives (named if known) that the person does or does not wish to have contact with.

■ Regulation 7 prescribes the information to be held in Part 2 of the Register (and Schedule 4 the form):

- the relative's name, address and date of birth;

- the name of the adoptee they wish to have contact with; or

- their wish not to have contact with a named adoptee.

■ Regulation 8 requires the Registrar General to give an adoptee named in Part 1 of the Register the name and contact address for any relative named in Part 2 of the Register who wishes to have contact.

■ Regulation 9 lays down fees of £15 for Part 1 of the Register (adoptees) and £30 for Part 2 (relatives).

■ Regulation 10 specifies that applicants for certified copies of entries in the Adopted Children Register relating to adopted children (i.e. under 18), must supply the:

- adopted child's full name and date of birth, and

- adopter's/adopters' full name/s.

■ An appropriate adoption agency (defined in section 65(1) of the Act) must apply in writing for information from the Register enabling an adoptee to obtain a copy of their birth certificate [reg.11].

■ Regulation 12 applies to pre-commencement adoptions and requires written applications for information necessary to enable adoptees over 18 to obtain a copy of their birth certificate.

■ Regulation 13 requires written applications for such information by adoptees under 18 who intend to marry or form a civil partnership.

■ Regulation 14 revokes previous regulations, except the Forms of Adoption Entry Regulations 1975 for pre-commencement adoptions, and the Registration of Foreign Adoption Regulations 2003 for certain inter-country adoptions.

Adoption Information and Intermediary Services (Pre-Commencement Adoptions) Regulations 2005

■ These regulations apply in England only and deal with assisting people adopted before 30.12.05 ('pre-commencement') to obtain information about their adoption and to facilitate contact with their birth relatives.

The Adoption Agencies Regulations 1983 continue to apply in relation to retention of case records for pre-commencement adoptions.

Disclosure of information about adoptions on or after 30.12.05 is dealt with by the Disclosure of Adoption Information (Post-Commencement Adoptions) Regulations 2005.

Intermediary services and intermediary agencies

- Intermediary services are defined by regulation 4 as:

  - assisting adopted people over 18 who were adopted pre-commencement to obtain information about their adoption, and

  - facilitating contact with their relatives.

- Adoption agencies which placed a person for adoption or hold their adoption information, and local authorities to which notice of a non-agency adoption was given, are referred to as 'the appropriate adoption agency' and are not deemed to be providing intermediary services if they only provide information on the adoption to that person [reg.4(2)].

- Adoption agencies and registered adoption support agencies providing intermediary services are 'intermediary agencies' for the purpose of the regulations [reg.4(3)].

- Regulation 3 stipulates that only adoption agencies and registered adoption support agencies may provide intermediary services and must do so in accordance with these regulations [reg.3(1) & (2)].

- Intermediary services are classed as an adoption support service [reg.3(3)].

- Intermediary agencies may accept applications to assist people adopted before 30.12.05 and their relatives to make contact, provided they are over 18 [reg.5(1) & (3)]. If the agency learns at any time that the subject of the application is under 18, it must not proceed further [reg.6(4)].

- Agencies must give priority to applications from people adopted before 12.11.75 and their relatives [reg.5(2)].

- Intermediary agencies are not required to proceed with applications if it would not be appropriate, having regard to:

- the welfare of the applicant, the subject [reg.6(2)(a)(i) & (ii)] and anyone who may be identified or affected (in particular anyone aged under 18) [reg.6(2)(a)(iii) & (3)];

- the views of the adoption agency [reg.6(2)(b)];

- information obtained from the Adoption Contact Register [reg.6(2)(c)];

- all the circumstances of the case [reg.6(2)].

Consent

- Agencies are required to obtain the subject's consent before disclosing identifying information [reg.7(1)] Identifying information is defined as that which on its own or with other known information enables the subject to be identified or traced [reg.7(4)].

- The agency must take all reasonable steps to obtain informed consent [reg.7(3)].

- If the subject is dead or incapable of giving informed consent, the agency may disclose identifying information if appropriate [regs.7(2) and 6(2)].

Veto on contact

- Regulation 8 enables an adoptee to write to register a veto with the appropriate agency preventing contact from intermediary agencies, or contact except in specified circumstances [reg.8(1)].

- The agency must record the veto on the adoptee's file and inform any intermediary agency which makes contact [reg.8(2)].

- Intermediary agencies must not proceed with an application if aware of a veto, except in specified circumstances [reg.8(3)].

- If the subject has not consented or a veto applies, non-identifying information may still be disclosed if the agency considers it appropriate [reg.9].

Counselling

- Intermediary agencies must provide written information about counselling, including providers and costs, to applicants and to subjects considering whether or not to consent, and must arrange it if requested [reg.10(1), (2) & (3)].

- Regulation 10(4) defines agencies which may provide counselling.

- Intermediary agencies must confirm the applicant's identity and age; that anyone acting for the applicant is authorised; and that any relative applying is related to the subject [reg.11].

- Intermediary agencies (unless the appropriate adoption agency) must take steps to identify any adoption agency which was involved in the adoption, including:

  • writing to the Registrar General;

  • writing to the court which made the order;

  • approaching the local authority where the adoption took place [reg.12(1) &(2)].

- The intermediary agency must then contact the identified adoption agency to find out if the subject has registered a veto or expressed any view about contact; seek the agency's views on the application; and ask for the information necessary to trace the subject, enable her/him to make an informed decision about consent, and provide counselling to the subject and the applicant [reg.12(3)].

- The appropriate adoption agency must provide the information requested unless a veto applies [reg.12(4)].

- Where there was no adoption agency involved, or the agency cannot be identified or does not hold the information, the intermediary agency (or the adoption agency if it does not hold the information) may write to the Registrar General for information [reg.13].

- The Registrar General must comply with the request or if she/he does not have the information, supply details of the court that made the adoption order [reg.14].

- The court must comply with any ensuing request or, if it does not have the information, supply details of any other court that may hold the information [reg.15].

- Regulation 16 requires information obtained or held under these regulations to be treated as confidential, and only disclosed in prescribed circumstances.

- Regulation 17 makes it an offence for an intermediary agency to disclose information without the subject's consent.

- Regulation 18 permits intermediary agencies and adoption agencies to charge reasonable fees.

- The Registrar General may charge £10 for providing information under regulation 14 [reg.18(3)].

- Courts may charge intermediary agencies up to £20 for providing information under regulation 15 [reg.18(4)].

Disclosure of Adoption Information (Post-Commencement Adoptions) Regulations 2005

- These regulations apply in England only and cover information to be kept by agencies and applications for disclosure of information relating to adoptions on or after 30.12.05 ('post-commencement').

Assistance with obtaining information about adoptions before 30.12.05 is dealt with by the Adoption Information and Intermediary Services (Pre-Commencement Adoptions) Regulations 2005.

- The adoption agency which placed the child or holds the records of the adoption [reg.3] must keep prescribed records, known as 'section 56 information' including the file set up in accordance with the Adoption Agencies Regulations 1983 or 2005 [reg.4(1) & (2)].

- Unless prejudicial to the adopted person's welfare or not reasonably practicable [reg.4(4)], the agency must keep:

  - anything supplied by a birth parent, relative or other significant person and intended to be given to the adopted person on request;

  - anything the adopted person has asked to be kept;

  - information from the Registrar General;

  - information from the Adoption Contact Register;

  - records made in compliance with regulations 10, 11, 14 & 18 (see below) [reg.4(3)].

- Section 56 information must be kept securely for at least 100 years after the adoption order, and be protected from theft, unauthorised disclosure, damage, loss and destruction [regs.5 & 6].

- Regulation 7 provides for transfer of section 56 records, on cessation of an agency's activity, to another agency (with approval of the registration authority), to the local authority where the agency (or its head office) is based, or to the resulting new agency if amalgamating. A voluntary agency must notify the local authority, where most activity took place, of the transfer. The receiving agency must notify the registration authority.

- Regulation 8 permits agencies to disclose section 56 information except 'protected information' [s.57(3) 2002 Act] for the purposes of carrying out its duties; and including protected information to another agency or support agency carrying out disclosure work, or to a researcher authorised by the Secretary of State.

■ Regulation 9 requires agencies to disclose section 56 information (including protected information) in various prescribed circumstances.

■ Agencies must record any information disclosed under Regulations 8 or 9, including what was disclosed, when, to whom and why [reg.10].

■ Regulation 11 provides for agreements as to the disclosure of protected information between an agency and:

  • anyone 18 or over in relation to information about them [reg.11(1)(a)]; and

  • adopters or parents who had parental responsibility before the adoption in relation to information about them or about the adopted person [reg.11(1)(b)].

■ Agreements must be in writing and include the names and signatures of the parties; the date; the reason for the agreement; and the information to be disclosed or any restrictions on the circumstances in which it may be disclosed [reg.11(2)].

■ An agency receiving an application for disclosure of protected information – which must be in writing and give reasons [reg.12] – must try to confirm the applicant's identity and that anyone acting on her/his behalf is authorised [reg.13].

■ Any views on disclosure obtained by the agency must be recorded [reg.14].

■ The following agency decisions are 'qualifying determinations' for the purposes of the Independent Review Mechanism (IRM) [s.12 2002 ACA]:

  • not to proceed with a disclosure application;

- to disclose information against the subject's wishes;

- not to disclose to the applicant information a person wishes to be disclosed [reg.15(1)].

■ The agency must advise the person in writing of the decision, the reasons for it, and the procedure for seeking an independent review [reg.15(2)].

■ On being notified of an application to the IRM, the agency must send to the Secretary of State within 10 working days:

- a copy of the disclosure application;

- a copy of the notice of its determination;

- a record of any views obtained by the agency;

- any other information the panel requests [reg.15(3)].

■ The agency must not act on its decision until the IRM panel has made a recommendation (and must take account of that recommendation before proceeding [reg.15(5)]) or for 40 days if no IRM application is made [reg.15(4)].

■ Regulations 6 and 7 clarify the definition of various terms.

■ Agencies must provide written information about available counselling and any fees charged to applicants for disclosure of information; anyone whose views about disclosure have been sought; and anyone making or considering an agreement under regulation 11, and arrange it on request [regs.16 & 17(1)].

■ Counselling may be provided by:

- the agency itself;

- an adoption agency or adoption support agency if the person is in England & Wales; a Scottish adoption agency if in Scotland; a registered adoption society or Board (defined by regulation 17(3)) if in Northern Ireland; or an equivalent person or body if outside the UK [reg.17(2)].

■ An agency may disclose information (including protected information) to a counsellor it has arranged under regulation 17, but must record any such disclosure in writing [reg.18].

■ If an agency does not hold information sought by an applicant over 18 who wishes to obtain a copy of her/his birth certificate, the agency must apply (paying any fee [reg.20(2)]) to the Registrar General for it, by supplying the:

• adoptee's name, date and country of birth;

• adopters' names; and

• date of the adoption order [reg.19].

■ Regulation 20 requires the Registrar General to disclose information required for a person to contact an adoption agency that holds her/his adoption records, and to disclose information from the Adoption Contact Register if asked by an agency dealing with a disclosure application.

■ Regulation 21 creates an offence by a voluntary agency of disclosing information in contravention of section 57 ACA 2002.

■ Regulation 22 permits agencies to charge reasonable fees for disclosing information; for providing counselling about disclosure; or for arranging such counselling outside the UK provided it has first given information about fees [reg.21(1) & (3)]; however, no fee may be charged to an adoptee for disclosure of information about her/his relatives and counselling connected with such disclosure [reg.22(2)].

Restriction on the Preparation of Adoption Reports Regulations 2005

- These regulations impose restrictions on the preparation of adoption reports under section 94(1) of the ACA 2002.

- Under regulation 3 those permitted to prepare adoption reports for the purposes of section 94(1) are:

  - social workers employed by an adoption agency who have at least three years' post-qualification child care experience including adoption, or supervised by an employee who meets this requirement; or

  - student social workers employed by or placed with an adoption agency and supervised by an employee who meets the experience requirement; or

  - social workers acting on the agency's behalf with the prescribed experience and supervised by an employee who meets the experience requirement.

  The interpretation of 'direct experience of adoption' is set out in the Guidance 1.53.

- The reports covered by the restrictions are:

  - a child's permanence report;

  - a prospective adopter's report;

  - an adoption placement report;

  - a report of an adoption placement visit (domestic adoptions);

  - a report of a visit or review (intercountry adoptions);

  - pre- and post-adoption reports i.e. reports produced for foreign authorities in connection with the adoption of a child from the relevant country.

• court reports on agency and non-agency cases, and on applications for parental responsibility prior to adoption abroad [reg.4].

Suitability of Adopters Regulations 2005

■ These regulations apply in England only and prescribe the matters an agency must take into account in determining the suitability of a prospective adopter.

■ Except where regulation 5 applies (see below), regulation 3 requires agencies to take account of the following in preparing prospective adopter's reports and review reports:

  • pre-assessment counselling;

  • preparation;

  • enhanced CRB check;

  • information required by Schedule 4 Part 1 Adoption Agencies Regulations 2005;

  • if applicable, any additional information about adopting from abroad [reg.15(4) Adoptions with a Foreign Element Regulations 2005];

  • medical report;

  • referee interview reports;

  • report from the adopter's local authority.

■ Except where regulation 5 applies (see below), agencies are required to take account of the following in reaching a decision as to a prospective adopter's suitability:

  • prospective adopter's report;

  • medical report;

- referee interview reports;

- panel recommendation;

- any additional information requested by the panel;

- if applicable, information about adopting from abroad (Part 3 Chapter 1 Adoptions with a Foreign Element Regulations 2005) [reg.4(1)].

■ In deciding on a couple's suitability, agencies must have proper regard to the stability and permanence of their relationship [reg.4(2)].

The statutory guidance 3.50–1 points to the practice guidance on assessment of prospective adopters for detailed advice on judging stability and permanence (at the time of going to press, the practice guidance is unpublished).

■ Regulation 5 applies where an agency receives information suggesting a prospective adopter may be unsuitable; in this case the agency may make its report and decision based only on the information collected up to that point.

Adoption Support Agencies (England) and Adoption Agencies (Miscellaneous Amendments) Regulations 2005

■ These regulations apply in England only and cover the provision of adoption support services by adoption support agencies under the Act, and for their regulation under the Care Standards Act 2000. Minor amendments to the Adoption Agencies Regulations 1983 (applicable only before 30.12.05) and the Adoption Information and Intermediary Services (Pre-commencement Adoptions) Regulations 2005 were included.

■ Regulation 2(2) clarifies that the term 'employee' covers volunteers and unpaid as well as paid workers.

■ Regulation 3 defines adoption support services as:

- counselling, advice and information;

- services for adoption by parents and their partners including support groups, help with contact, therapy, training and respite (if including accommodation, subject to sections 23 or 59 Children Act 1989 [reg.3(2)]) and other services which maintain the adoption, and help with or to prevent disruption;

- helping agencies prepare and train adopters;

- help with contact for adopted adults and their relatives and former relatives.

■ Regulation 4 excludes from being considered adoption support agencies:

- lawyers providing a service as part of their practice;

- anyone just running discussion groups in relation to adoption;

- registered homes or agencies providing respite or day care including as adoption support.

■ Adoption support agencies are required to produce and review a Statement of Purpose and (if services are provided to children) a Children's Guide and provide copies for the registration authority, staff and service users. The Children' Guide must be in a form suitable for the comprehension and ages of children served by the agency. The agency must act in accordance with its Statement of Purpose [reg.5 & 6].

■ A person running an agency must:

- be of good character, physically and mentally fit;

- not be bankrupt;

- supply the checks, references and information listed in Schedule 2 [reg.7].

■ Organisations or partnerships, or anyone unfit or not wishing to run the agency, must appoint a suitably qualified and experienced manager who meets the requirements, and advise the registration authority [reg.8 & 9].

- The person running the agency must do so with care, competence and skill, and must undertake regular training [reg.10].

- Regulation 11 requires the manager or person running the agency to supply written details of any criminal conviction immediately to the registration authority.

- Agencies providing services to children must have a child protection policy and procedure which includes:

  - what to do about allegations of abuse or neglect;

  - liaison and co-operation with local authorities;

  - how to contact relevant local authorities and the registration authority about any concern [reg.12].

- Regulation 13 requires services to be appropriate to the person's assessed needs.

- Regulation 14 stipulates the information to be held in records and allows the agency discretion as to how long to maintain them.

- Adoption support agencies holding records of pre-commencement adoptions (before 30.12.05) have the same obligations as adoption agencies in relation to storage, retention, transfer and disclosure of information from those records [reg.15].

- Agencies must have a complaints procedure for service users (including people refused a service) and must supply a copy to staff, and on request to service users and anyone acting on a child's behalf [reg.16].

- Complaints must be fully investigated, within 28 days where practicable, and the complainant advised of the outcome and any resulting action [reg.17(1) & (2)].

- Records of the complaint, investigation, outcome and action taken must be kept for three years [reg.17(3)].

- Agencies must enable children to complain, and ensure there are no reprisals for making a complaint [reg.17(4)].

- Agencies must supply the registration authority on request a summary of the previous year's complaints and action taken [reg.17(5)].

- Agencies must have enough suitably qualified and experienced staff for their statement of purpose and to meet the needs of services users [reg.18].

- Staff must:

  - be of good character, physically and mentally fit; have the necessary qualifications, skills and experience; supply the checks, references and information listed in Schedule 2 [reg.19];

  - be appointed subject to a probationary period; given a job description; receive training, supervision and appraisal; be enabled to gain appropriate further qualifications [reg.20].

- Agencies must have a disciplinary procedure, which includes suspension of staff to safeguard service users and makes it a disciplinary matter not to report actual or suspected abuse of a child [reg.21].

- Agencies must keep staff records covering the information specified in Schedule 3 for a period of at least 15 years from date of last entry [reg.22].

- Premises must be suitable in accordance with the agency's statement of purpose and must provide secure storage for records; records stored off the premises must also be kept securely [reg.23].

- Regulation 24 requires the agency to notify the bodies set out in Schedule 4 of the death of or serious injury to a child receiving a service, or the registration authority where a member of staff is referred for inclusion on the Protection of Children Act 1999 list held by the Secretary of State. Verbal notification must be confirmed in writing within 14 days.

- Regulations 25–28 cover the requirements in relation to financial and managerial stability and action in the event of specified circumstances.

- Regulation 29 makes it an offence to fail to comply with certain of the regulations.

- Where more than one person is responsible for a required action, only one of them need do it to comply with the regulation [reg.30].

- Regulations 31–33 amend the National Care Standards Commission (Registration) Regulations 2001, the National Care Standards Commission (Fees and Frequency of Inspections) (Adoption Agencies) Regulations 2003 and the Commission for Social Care Inspection (Fees and Frequency of Inspections) Regulations 2004 to include adoption support agencies.

- Regulation 35 amends Regulation 4 of the Adoption Information and Intermediary Services (Pre-Commencement Adoptions) Regulations 2005 to enable an adoption support agency to provide information to an adopted person from records it holds without being deemed to be providing an intermediary service.

Special Guardianship Regulations 2005

- These regulations apply in England only and relate to provision by local authorities of services to support special guardianship orders.

- Local authorities are required to provide or ensure the provision of counselling, advice and information in relation to special guardianship (section 14F Children Act 1989) and the following prescribed services:

- financial support (see regulations 6–10);

- groups for children, their parents, special guardians and prospective special guardians;

- assistance, including mediation, with contact between children and their parents, relatives and others if beneficial to the child's welfare;

- therapeutic services for the child; and

- support services including training, respite care and mediation [reg.3(1)].

■ Regulation 3(2) permits any of the prescribed services to include cash assistance.

■ Regulation 3(3) clarifies that any respite care accommodation must comply with sections 23 or 59 Children Act 1989.

■ Special guardianship support services may be provided by adoption agencies, adoption support agencies, registered fostering agencies, health bodies and education authorities [reg.4].

■ Local authorities may provide special guardianship support services outside their area [reg.5(3)], and must do so for three years from the date of the order for:

- a child they are – or were immediately before the order – looking after;

- the special guardian or prospective special guardian of such a child;

- the children of such special guardians or prospective special guardians [reg.5(1) & (2)].

■ The cut-off period of three years does not apply to financial support agreed before the order was made [reg.5(2)].

- Regulation 6 provides that financial support may be paid to:

  - prospective special guardians to help them become a child's special guardian where this would benefit the child's welfare, or

  - support special guardians in such cases after the order has been made [reg.6(1)].

- Regulation 6(2) sets out the circumstances in which financial support may be paid:

  - to enable a special guardian or prospective special guardian to look after a child;

  - where a child needs greater expenditure on special care because of illness, disability, emotional or behavioural difficulty, or past abuse or neglect;

  - to cover legal costs (including court fees) for a special guardianship application, a section 8 (Children Act 1989) application, or an order for financial provision for the child;

  - to contribute to the child's accommodation and maintenance, including furniture and equipment, house alterations, transport, clothes, toys and other necessary items.

- Financial support can only include a reward element if agreed in advance of the order where the special guardian or prospective special guardian was the child's foster carer and was receiving payments including a reward element for the child [reg.7(1)].

- The reward element is payable for up to two years from the order unless the child has exceptional needs or there are exceptional circumstances [reg.7(2)].

- Financial support may be paid periodically to meet recurring expenses (subject to the conditions in regulation 10(1)), in a lump sum, or in agreed instalments [reg.8].

- Under regulation 9, financial support ends when the child:

  - is no longer with the special guardian;

  - finishes full-time education and starts work;

  - qualifies for state benefits;

  - reaches 18, unless continuing in full-time education, when it can continue until the course ends.

- In order to receive periodic payments of financial support, the special guardian or prospective special guardian must agree to:

  - notify the local authority immediately (and if orally, confirm in writing in seven days) of any new address, the child's death, any changes listed in regulation 9 and any change in financial circumstances or the financial needs or resources of the child;

  - supply an annual statement of financial circumstances and the financial needs and resources of the child, plus confirmation of address and that the child is still there [reg.10(1)].

- Local authorities may impose conditions on payments, including how and when they are to be spent [reg.10(2)].

- Payments may be suspended or stopped if any conditions are not met, and the local authority may seek repayment of part or all of the amount paid; however, in the case of failure to supply an annual statement, the authority must first send a reminder giving 28 days to comply [reg.10(3) & (4)].

- Local authorities must assess support needs at the request of a child who is (or was immediately before a special guardianship order) looked after, a special guardian or prospective special guardian of such a child, or a parent of such a child [reg.11(1)].

- Local authorities may assess support needs on receiving a written request from (or if a child, on behalf of):

- a child on a special guardianship order (or the subject of an application);

- a special guardian (or an applicant);

- a parent;

- a special guardian's child;

- anyone with a significant ongoing relationship with the child [reg.11(2)].

■ If minded not to assess where it has discretion, a local authority must advise the applicant with reasons, and give them a reasonable opportunity to make representations [reg.11(3)].

■ Assessments may be limited to a particular support service if it is specifically requested or seems the most appropriate provision [reg.11(4)].

■ Assessments must consider any of the following which are relevant:

- the child's development needs;

- the special guardian/prospective special guardian's parenting capacity;

- the child's family and background;

- the child's life with the special guardian/prospective special guardian;

- any previous assessments;

- the special guardian/prospective special guardian's needs and those of their family;

- the likely effect of a special guardianship order on relationships between the child, the parent and the special guardian/prospective special guardian [reg.12(1)].

■ The local authority must, if appropriate, interview the subject of any assessment and, if a child, also interview the special guardian/prospective special guardian or any other appropriate adult [reg.12(2)].

- If health or education services appear to be needed, the relevant body must be consulted as part of the assessment [reg.12(3)].

- Local authorities must write a report of the assessment. [reg.12(4)].

- In deciding an amount of financial support, local authorities must take account of any grant, benefit, allowance or resource available to the person as a special guardian/prospective special guardian [reg.13(2)].

- Unless regulation 13(4) or (5) applies, local authorities must also take account of:

  - the person's financial resources, including state benefits payable for the child;

  - the person's reasonable outgoings and commitments (excluding the child);

  - the child's financial needs and resources [reg.13(3)].

- Under regulation 13(4) local authorities must disregard the means test in regulation 13(3) if paying legal costs to support a special guardianship application for a looked after child.

- Regulation 13(5) allows local authorities to disregard the regulation 13(3) means test when paying:

  - setting up or special care costs for a child they looked after;

  - ongoing travel costs for contact purposes;

  - any reward element under regulation 7 [reg.13(5)].

- Except for advice and information or one-off support, local authorities must draw up a support services plan [reg.14(2)].

- If health or education services appear to be needed, the relevant body must be consulted before drawing up the plan [reg.14(3)].

- Local authorities must nominate someone to monitor the plan's implementation [reg.14(4)].

- People must be given the chance to make representations before a decision about support needs is made, having first been notified of the proposed decision and the time allowed for making representations [reg.15(1) & (2)].

- The notice must state:

  - the person's support needs;

  - the basis for determining any financial support and the amount payable;

  - if the local authority proposes to provide any support services and, if so, which services;

  - any conditions to be imposed [reg.15(3)].

- If services are to be provided and a plan is required, a draft plan must accompany the notice [reg.15(4)].

- No decision can be made until:

  - the person has made representations or accepted the proposal and any draft plan, or

  - the time limit has expired [reg.15(5)].

- When the local authority has made a decision about providing support services, it must notify the person, with reasons [reg.16(1)].

- If a plan is required, the notice must include the plan and the person nominated to monitor it [reg.16(2)].

- For financial support, the notice must state:

  - how the amount is calculated;

- the amount, frequency, period and start date of payments by instalments;

- the date of any one-off payment;

- any conditions attached, any date by which they are to be met and what happens if they are not met;

- review, variation and termination procedures;

- the local authority's and special guardian or prospective special guardian's respective responsibilities with regard to reviews [reg.16(3)].

■ Reviews of periodic financial support are covered by regulation 18 and of other services by regulation 17.

■ Regulation 17(2) requires the local authority to review provision at least annually; and if the person's circumstances change; and at any other time appropriate to the plan.

■ Reviews must be conducted as for assessments in accordance with regulations 12 and 13 [reg.17(3)].

■ People must be given the chance to make representations before a decision about variation or termination of support services is made, having first been notified of the proposed decision and the time allowed for making representations. The notice must contain the information listed in regulation 15(3) and any revised draft plan [reg.17(4) & (5)].

■ Local authorities must make a decision about variation or termination based on the review and any representations, and if necessary revise the plan; they must then notify the person, with reasons and details of any revised plan [reg.17(6) & (7)].

■ Regulation 18(2) requires local authorities to review financial support on receipt of the annual statement; and if the person's circumstances change or any condition is breached; and at any other time appropriate to the plan.

- Reviews must be conducted as for assessments in accordance with regulations 12 and 13 [reg.18(4)].

- People must be given the chance to make representations before a decision to reduce or stop payments or revise the plan, having first been notified of the proposed decision and the time allowed for making representations. The notice must contain the information listed in regulation 15(3) and any revised draft plan [reg.18(5) & 7)].

- Payments may be suspended pending a decision [reg.18(6)].

- Local authorities must make a decision about variation, termination or recovery of any payments made, based on the review and any representations, and if necessary revise the plan; they must then notify the person, with reasons and details of any revised plan [reg.18(8) & (9)].

- In urgent cases, the local authority may disregard any requirement to assess, plan or notify which would delay service provision [reg.19].

- Regulation 20 requires notices to be in writing and, in the case of a child who is not of sufficient age or understanding or where the local authority deems it inappropriate, to be given to the special guardian or prospective special guardian or other appropriate adult.

- Regulation 21 prescribes the content of court reports in special guardianship cases as set out in Schedule 1.

- Regulation 22 clarifies that the local authority responsible under section 24 (leaving care provisions) Children Act 1989 for a child subject to a special guardianship order is the one which last looked after the child.

Part III

National Minimum Standards

National Minimum Standards Adoption Agencies

- These standards, effective from 30.04.03 (and amended 30.12.05), are issued under section 23(1) and section 49(1) Care Standards Act 2000. They apply to voluntary adoption agencies in England and Wales and local authorities in England.

- Though not enforceable in themselves, they will be used by the registration authorities (Commission for Social Care Inspection in England and National Assembly for Wales) when registering and inspecting adoption agencies to determine whether the agencies meet their obligations under the (mandatory) regulations.

VALUES STATEMENT

- Children are entitled to grow up as part of a loving family which can meet their needs during childhood and beyond.

- It is best for children where possible to be brought up by their own birth family.

- The child's welfare, safety and needs will be at the centre of the adoption process.

- The child's wishes and feelings will be actively sought and fully taken into account at all stages.

- Delays in adoption can have a severe impact on the health and development of children and should be avoided wherever possible.

- Children's ethnic origin, cultural background, religion and language will be fully recognised and positively valued and promoted when decisions are made.

- The particular needs of disabled children will be fully recognised and taken into account when decisions are made.

- The role of adoptive parents in offering a permanent family to a child who cannot live with their birth family will be valued and respected.

- Adoption has lifelong implications for all involved and requires lifelong commitment from many different organisations, professionals and individuals who have to work together to meet the needs for services of those affected by adoption.

- Government will work in partnership with local government, other statutory agencies and voluntary adoption agencies to ensure that these standards are delivered.

STATEMENT OF PURPOSE

Outcome: There is a clear written statement of the aims and objectives of the agency and the agency ensures that it meets those aims and objectives.

Standard 1: Statement of purpose

There is a written statement of the agency's aims and objectives, describing its facilities and services.

The statement must be formally approved and reviewed at least annually.

The statement includes:

- status and constitution (voluntary agencies only);
- organisation and control;
- functions (local authorities only).

Local authorities and agencies which provide adoption support services to children must produce a children's guide which:

- is suitable for all children (if necessary in different formats);

- is given to children as soon as an adoption decision is made;

- summarises each stage (including court) and how long each takes;

- explains how to get an independent advocate, how to make a complaint and how to contact the Children's Rights Director or Children's Commissioner for Wales.

Oral or written communications must be available in accessible formats for children, birth parents/guardians, prospective/adopters and staff with disabilities, and if necessary read, translated or explained to them.

The agency's policies, procedures and any guidance must reflect the statement of purpose.

Agency staff are aware of the statement of purpose and a copy is readily available.

SECURING AND PROMOTING CHILDREN'S WELFARE
Outcome: The needs and wishes, welfare and safety of the child are at the centre of the adoption process.

Standard 2: Matching

The agency has written plans for recruiting sufficient adopters for the children waiting for adoption locally.

Children are matched with adopters who best meet their assessed needs, if possible with a family which:

- reflects their ethnic origin, cultural background, religion and language; and

- allows them to live with brothers and sisters unless this will not meet their individual needs.

Where these two requirements cannot be met, a clear explanation is given to the child and recorded.

Where the child cannot be matched with a family which reflects their ethnic origin, cultural background, religion and language, every effort must be made to find a suitable family within a realistic time-scale so that the child does not wait indefinitely.

Matches of children with adopters take account of:

- the child's views;

- the child's care plan;

- recent written assessments of the child and his or her birth family, potential adopters and their children.

PROSPECTIVE AND APPROVED ADOPTERS

Outcome: The agency recruits and supports sufficient adopters from diverse backgrounds, who can offer children a stable and permanent home to achieve a successful and lasting placement.

Standard 3: Information

Plans for recruitment will specify that prospective adopters will be welcomed without prejudice, given clear information, and will be treated fairly, openly and with respect.

Eligibility criteria, information and what is expected of adopters is provided on request. Overseas adopters are also given information about laws or criteria for adoption in the overseas country, the processes that they must follow, the countries they may adopt from, and the eligibility criteria of those countries.

The agency has a system for prioritising the prospective adopters most likely to meet the needs of children waiting.

Voluntary agencies only where there are specific eligibility criteria, e.g. religion, or prospective adopters do not meet the needs of local children waiting, applicants are told at the beginning and, if necessary, referred to another agency.

Applicants have information about preparation and support services, and the opportunity to talk to other adopters.

Information is given about children who need families locally and nationally.

Standard 4: Assessment and preparation

There is a formal, thorough and comprehensive assessment, preparation and approval process.

The preparation programme is made available to all prospective adopters, including overseas adopters.

Preparation follows equal opportunities and anti-discriminatory practice and is organised to encourage attendance (e.g. time and venue).

Preparation is evaluated and reviewed annually.

Existing foster carers of the child they wish to adopt are entitled to the same information and preparation as other prospective adopters.

Applicants' ability to look after children safely and meet their needs is considered.

Preparation is sensitive and covers the issues adopters are likely to encounter and the competencies and strengths they need.

Status, health and enhanced Criminal Records Bureau (CRB) checks, personal references and enquiries are undertaken about prospective adopters, enhanced CRB checks are undertaken on household members aged over 17, and reasons for these checks are explained.

Prospective adopters are kept informed of progress.

Standard 5: Matching

Adopters are given clear written information about matching, introduction and placement, and any support they may need, including the role of the Adoption Register.

Before a match is agreed, adopters have accurate, up-to-date and full written information on the needs and background of the child and an opportunity to discuss this and the implications for them and their family.

The agency has a system to:

- ask adopters if they agree to notify the agency if the child dies during childhood or soon afterwards;

- explain the importance for the birth family of this information; and

- pass on the information to the birth parents if they want it.

Records are kept of the adopters' decision and subsequent action.

Appropriate information is obtained for the child from the prospective adopters about them, their home and any children, family and pets.

Standard 6: Adopters – support

Adopters are helped and supported to provide stable and permanent homes for the children placed with them.

The agency has a strategy for supporting adopters, including preparing them in advance of the child coming to live with them.

The agency offers information, support and advice to prospective adopters who receive a proposed match with a child from overseas.

The agency explains to adopters the importance of keeping safe any information from birth families and encourages them to provide this to the child on request, or when appropriate.

The agency helps adopters to understand and help the child deal with racism or other discrimination.

The agency explains to adopters that, to help the child develop and maintain a positive self-identity, they need to help and encourage the child to understand his or her history, and keep appropriate memorabilia.

Where there are difficulties in a placement or if it disrupts, the agencies involved co-operate to provide information and support to adopters and child.

BIRTH PARENTS AND BIRTH FAMILIES
Outcome: Birth parents are entitled to services that recognise the lifelong implications of adoption. They will be treated fairly, openly and with respect throughout the adoption process.

Standard 7: Involvement in adoption plans

The service to birth parents recognises the lifelong implications of adoption.

The agency works with birth parents to plan effectively for their child/ren.

Birth parents' views about adoption and contact are clearly recorded.

Local authorities only ensure birth parents have a support worker independent of the child's social worker from when adoption is identified as the plan.

Birth parents see and can comment on what is written about them or their circumstances before information is passed to the adoption panel or adopters.

Standard 8: Maintaining the child's heritage

Birth parents and birth families are enabled to contribute to the maintenance of their child's heritage.

Efforts are made to obtain for the child clear information from birth parents and birth families about themselves and life before the child's adoption, including the child's birth and early life, the birth family's view about adoption and contact and up-to-date information about themselves and their situation.

Standard 9: Support

The agency has a strategy for working with and supporting birth parents and birth families (including siblings) before and after adoption including giving information about support groups and services and helping birth parents to fulfil agreed contact plans.

ADOPTION PANELS AND AGENCY DECISIONS

Outcome: 1. Each agency has an adoption panel which is organised efficiently and is effective in making quality and appropriate recommendations about children suitable for adoption, the suitability of prospective adopters and the matching of children and approved adopters.

2. The agency's decisions are made to promote and safeguard the welfare of children.

Standard 10: Functions of adoption panels

Adoption panels have clear written policies and procedures about their functions and ensure they are implemented.

The policies and procedures include as a minimum:

- appointment of Chair and Vice-chair;
- dealing with ineffective or disruptive behaviour and attitudes;
- declaring an interest in a case;
- ensuring the panel is quorate;
- decision-making when panel members disagree;
- emergency panel meetings for urgent placements;
- feedback to the agency on the quality of cases presented to panel;
- promotion of good practice, consistency of approach and fairness by panel members; and
- progress reports on individual cases.

Prospective adopters can attend panel and be heard.

Standard 11: Constitution and membership

The agency ensures that each adoption panel is properly constituted, panel members have suitable qualities and experience and have regular training to keep up to date with changes in law, guidance and practice. Where the agency is involved in intercountry adoption, each panel member understands the implications of a child being adopted from overseas and seeks advice, when necessary, on laws and eligibility criteria for the overseas country.

The agency allows each new panel member to observe an adoption panel.

No panel member begins work until CRB and status checks are satisfactorily completed and they have signed a confidentiality agreement.

The agency ensures that:

- each panel member has induction training within 10 weeks of becoming a member;

- there is an annual joint training day with the agency's adoption staff;

- members have access to appropriate training and skills development;

- members are kept abreast of changes to legislation, regulation and guidance; and

- members receive training in the basic principles of law and eligibility criteria for overseas adoption, where the agency provides an intercountry adoption service.

Standard 12: Timeliness

Adoption panels are efficiently organised and conducted, and are convened regularly to avoid any delays in consideration of prospective adopters and matching children and adopters.

Panel members receive all necessary information on the prospective/approved adopters and children in advance of the panel.

The minutes of panel meetings accurately cover the panel's discussion, reasons for conclusions reached, and recommendations made.

Standard 13: Agency decision

The agency's decision is made without delay, taking into account the recommendation of the adoption panel and promotes and safeguards the welfare of the child.

The decision-maker takes into account all the information surrounding the case and the panel's recommendation before making a decision.

The agency conveys its decision orally to the child, and in writing to the parents or guardian and prospective/approved adopters, as appropriate.

FITNESS TO PROVIDE OR MANAGE AN AGENCY

Outcome: The agency is provided and managed by those with the appropriate skills and experience to do so efficiently and effectively and by those who are suitable to work with children.

Standard 14: Skills to carry on or manage

The people involved in running and managing the agency:

- have enough knowledge and experience of child care and adoption law and practice; and

- have management skills and financial expertise; and

- ensure it is run in a financially sound and professional way.

The manager has:

- a professional qualification relevant to a child care setting, which must be Care NVQ level 4, DipSW or professional social work equivalent; and

- by 01.04.05, a qualification at level 4 NVQ in management or another qualification matching the NVQ Level 4 competencies required; and

- by 01.04.05, at least two years' experience in a child care setting, which may include managing a voluntary agency or a local authority adoption service, within the past five years.

In voluntary adoption agencies only, the branch manager has:

- a professional qualification relevant to working with children, which must be either Care NVQ level 4, DipSW or professional equivalent; and

- by 01.04.05, at least two years' experience in a child care setting, which may include managing a branch of a voluntary agency or a local authority adoption service, within the five years.

In voluntary adoption agencies providing adoption support services only, the branch manager has:

- a professional qualification relevant to working in child care, which must be either Care NVQ level 4, DipSW or professional equivalent; or

- a recognised counselling/therapy accreditation; and

- by 30.12.07, at least two years' experience in a child care setting, which may include managing an adoption support agency, a branch of a voluntary agency or a local authority adoption service, within the past five years.

The manager exercises effective leadership so that the agency delivers the best possible child care.

The manager has a clear written job description covering duties, responsibilities and level of delegation, and specifies the person to whom the manager is accountable. Any change in the person to whom they are accountable must be notified in writing to the manager.

Standard 15: Suitability to carry on or manage

Anyone running or managing the agency is suitable to run a voluntary organisation or business concerned with safeguarding and promoting children's welfare.

Written references are verified by telephone enquiries.

The manager must have a satisfactory enhanced CRB disclosure.

CRB checks are renewed every three years.

PROVISION AND MANAGEMENT OF THE AGENCY
Outcome: The agency is organised and managed efficiently, delivering a good quality service and avoiding confusion and conflicts of role.

Standard 16: Managing effectively and efficiently

The agency is managed effectively and efficiently.

The agency ensures it is run in line with its Statement of Purpose.

Someone else takes charge when the manager is absent.

Managers and staff have clear roles, lines of communication and accountability.

The agency informs managers and staff that they must declare possible conflicts of interest.

The agency ensures that staff who work with children, prospective/approved adopters and birth parents, take into account and respect:

- their racial origin, religion, culture, language, sexuality, gender and disability;
- the familiarity with adoption of prospective adopters;
- the experience and understanding of adoption of birth parents.

The agency has procedures covering the use of the Adoption Register for England and Wales, including providing information to the Register about:

- children who have an adoption plan and any care proceedings have been completed, and
- approved adopters waiting for children.

Standard 17: Monitoring and controlling

There are procedures for monitoring and controlling the activities of the agency and ensuring quality performance.

Information is given to purchasers of services and others, including:

- service charges;
- any amounts paid to adopters; and
- itemised amounts paid for services.

The agency's governing body:

- is satisfied that the agency is effective and achieves good outcomes for children;
- receives written reports every six months to monitor progress; and
- for voluntary agencies, ensures all registration conditions are met.

Standard 18: Specialist advisers

The agency has specialist advisers and services appropriate to its needs.

A medical adviser is available for consultation and is a member of the panel. The medical adviser can access specialist medical advice on the agency's behalf.

There is a legal adviser available for consultation by staff and the panel.

The agency can access other specialisms according to its needs, including on race and culture, and adopting from another country.

There is a protocol governing specialist advisers, who should be suitably qualified and, where applicable, registered by a professional body.

EMPLOYMENT AND MANAGEMENT OF STAFF
Outcome: The people who work in the agency are suitable to work with children and young people (and users of adoption support services where

provided) and are managed, trained and supported in such a way as to ensure the best possible outcomes for children waiting to be adopted or who have been adopted (and users of adoption support services where provided). The number of staff and their range of qualifications and experience are sufficient to achieve the purposes and functions of the agency.

Standard 19: Suitability to work with children

Anyone working for the agency is suitable to work with children and young people and to safeguard and promote their welfare.

There are recruitment and selection procedures which follow good practice in safeguarding children and young people, and which all those responsible for recruitment and selection of staff are trained in, understand and operate.

All people working for the agency are interviewed and have written references checked before taking up their duties. Written references are verified with telephone enquiries.

All people working for the agency, including on a temporary, sessional or voluntary basis have a satisfactory standard or enhanced CRB disclosure, as appropriate.

No person begins work without confirmation that all status, CRB and reference checks are satisfactory.

CRB checks for current staff which need to be updated (three years or more since the last check) remain effective.

QUALIFICATIONS
Social workers

All social workers have a DipSW or equivalent qualification and a good understanding of adoption.

By 01.04.06, at least 20% of the agency's social workers should have or be obtaining the PQ Child Care Award.

Social workers have appropriate knowledge and skills, including:

- relevant law, guidance, policies and procedures (listed);

- assessing prospective adopters;

- children's growth and development and the effect of neglect, abuse and loss;

- communicating with children and young people;

- understanding the importance of a complaints procedure;

- promoting equality, diversity and the rights of individuals and groups; and

- the roles of other agencies, in particular, health and education.

Social workers assessing adopters have at least three years' post qualification experience in child care, including direct experience recruiting, preparing, assessing and supporting adopters. Students and others who do not meet this requirement only carry out assessments if the responsible supervisor does.

Other professional staff

All advisers and professional staff are qualified and trained to work with children and young people, their families and adopters, and have a good understanding of adoption.

Other staff

Unqualified staff carrying out social work functions only do so if directly supervised by qualified social workers who check and are accountable for their work.

Any support workers for birth parents have knowledge and understanding of adoption and their work is supervised by a social worker.

Adoption support service – counsellors and therapists

In local authorities and agencies providing adoption support services:

- counsellors (except those providing birth records counselling) and therapists have appropriate accreditation (from bodies as listed);
- birth records counselling is by qualified social workers trained and experienced in this type of counselling and with a thorough understanding of the law on access to birth records and the impact of reunion.

Standard 20: Organisation and management of staff

Staff are organised and managed in a way which delivers an efficient and effective service.

Staff are managed and monitored by those with appropriate skills and qualifications.

Levels of management delegation and responsibility are defined and appropriate for the skills, qualifications and experience of the relevant members of staff.

The agency can determine, prioritise and monitor workloads and assign tasks to appropriate staff.

The agency ensures that assessments and approvals of prospective adopters are managed effectively.

Regular professional supervision and consultation are provided for social workers by suitable staff.

Staff undertake ongoing training and professional and skills development.

The agency has adequate clerical and administrative support, office equipment, and infrastructure to enable staff to work efficiently and effectively.

The agency can deal promptly and courteously with enquiries from prospective adopters and other service users.

There is enough advice to provide a full service for children and young people and to support prospective/approved adopters, including childcare, medical, educational and other professional and legal advice.

Employees, sessional workers and consultants have written contracts, job descriptions and conditions of service complying with the General Social Care Council (England) (GSCC) or Care Council for Wales (CCW) code of practice.

Staff have a copy of the:

- statement of purpose;
- grievance and disciplinary policies and procedures;
- services offered;
- equal opportunities policy;
- health and safety procedures;
- complaint procedure;
- GSCC's or CCW's Code of Practice;
- child protection policy, where support services are provided to children.

Standard 21: Sufficient staff with the right skills/experience

There are enough experienced and qualified staff to meet the needs of the agency and they are supported and assisted in providing a service.

The staffing complement (numbers, grades, experience and qualifications) is adequate to meet, at all times, the agency's needs and Statement of Purpose.

There are short- and long-term contingency plans to resolve shortfalls in staffing.

Staff retention is encouraged, by providing support, training, flexible working conditions, supervision, study leave, clear workloads and terms and conditions.

Standard 22: Fair and competent employer

The agency is a fair and competent employer, with sound employment practices and good support for staff.

The agency has public liability and professional indemnity insurance for staff. For voluntary agencies only, the policy covers costs arising as a result of child abuse claims against staff.

There is a whistle-blowing policy made known to all staff.

Standard 23: Training

There is good quality training to enhance individual skills and to keep staff up to date with professional and legal developments.

There is a plan for ongoing training and appropriate professional and skills development of staff doing child care and adoption/adoption support work through induction, NVQ, post-qualifying and in-service training. All new staff have induction training starting within seven days and completed within six weeks linked to TOPSS Induction Standards in England or in line with the CCW induction framework in Wales.

An appraisal or review scheme identifies training and development needs of staff doing adoption work. Individual training programmes are available, outcomes are monitored and linked to staff needs assessment, and relate to assigned tasks.

The agency keeps staff abreast of changes in legislation, guidance and case law and enables them to attend regular staff/team meetings and discuss current practice.

Staff training is routinely evaluated and reviewed at least annually.

Training reflects the policies and legal obligations of the agency.

Standard 24: Right to make a complaint (voluntary agencies only)

Complaints are resolved quickly and handled sensitively, thoroughly and impartially.

The agency advises staff and all involved with the agency, including those refused a service, of their right to make a complaint. Procedures help children to complain.

The complaint procedure is given to staff and is readily available on request.

The complaints procedure:

• includes how to make a complaint;

• does not restrict what may be complained about;

- specifies how complaints will be handled;

- provides information on other complaints procedures, e.g. of local authorities, CSCI's Children's Rights Director, Care Standards Inspectorate for Wales, National Commissioner for Local Administration and Children's Commissioner for Wales;

- is accessible to disabled people and those whose first language is not English.

Complaints are handled seriously and promptly.

Staff are trained in the complaints procedures, including:

- what constitutes a complaint;

- how to deal with a complaint and record it;

- to whom a complaint may be made outside the agency;

- what to do if a complaint is not resolved promptly by informal means, including whom to notify and what to record; and

- how to help a child complain.

The agency keeps a record of complaints, how they are dealt with and the outcome.

The agency reviews the records at least annually to check the procedure is working, identify any patterns and take action on individual complaints.

Any action from such a review is appropriate in relation to its policies and practices and in relation to individual cases. A record is made of action taken.

RECORDS
Note: Local authority adoption services may keep some records separately and duplicate records are not required by this standard.

Outcome: All appropriate records are maintained securely, kept and are accessible when required.

Standard 25: Case records for children and prospective/approved adopters

The agency maintains comprehensive and accurate case records for each child and adopter with whom the agency has worked.

The agency has written instructions to:

- cover confidentiality of adoption information and adoption case records and their indexes; and

- ensure indexes and case records for children and adopters are securely stored to minimise risk of fire or water damage.

Staff, panel members and specialist advisers understand the instructions and compliance is monitored.

Records are kept of status, health and CRB checks, enquiries and written references obtained for adopters, and CRB checks obtained for household members aged over 17, and their outcomes.

The record-keeping system is congruent with the Looked After Children System/Integrated Children's System.

Supervisors' decisions are recorded on case files and are legible, clear, signed and dated.

Standard 26: Access to records

The agency gives information from its case files promptly to other adoption agencies and local authorities to effect the placement of a child.

The agency's instructions take account of the Data Protection Act and

Human Rights Act and cover:

- authorising access to adoption case records and their indexes and disclosure of adoption information;

- when to make records or information available under the Adoption Agencies Regulations 1983 and 2005;

- how to deal with requests for access or disclosure and who can authorise them;

- the requirement for a written confidentiality agreement before disclosure (this does not cover the child or adopter but covers anyone else in or outside the agency, including the adoption panel).

Standard 27: Administrative records

There is a case recording policy covering the purpose, format, confidentiality and contents of files, including secure storage and access to files, in line with regulations.

Separate records are kept on those working for the agency, complaints and allegations.

The quality and adequacy of records are monitored and necessary action is taken.

Confidential records are always stored securely and there is a policy on access.

Written entries in records are legible, clear, non-stigmatising, signed and dated and distinguish between fact, opinion and third party information.

There is a system for keeping complaints records and handling them confidentially and securely. Records of complaints and allegations are clearly recorded on files for staff, prospective/approved adopters, birth parents, birth family and children, including investigation, conclusion and action taken. Separate records are also kept which bring together data on allegations and on complaints.

Standard 28: Personnel files for members of staff and members of adoption panels

Up-to-date, comprehensive files are kept for staff and members of the panel.

Records are kept of:

- qualifications;

- status and CRB checks, enquiries and references and their outcomes;

- experience in a childcare setting;

- training;

- complaints made against staff or members of the adoption panel;

- disciplinary action.

CRB checks are renewed every three years.

FITNESS OF PREMISES
Outcome: The premises used by the agency are suitable for the purpose.

Standard 29: Premises

Premises used by the agency are appropriate for the purpose.

Office premises are identifiable and accessible during normal office hours.

Administration, including IT and communications, is efficient and robust. Premises have:

- a lockable room for secure records retention;

- safeguards for IT systems; and

- appropriate security.

The premises and contents are adequately insured (or can be promptly replaced).

The agency has a Disaster Recovery Plan covering provision of premises and safeguarding/back-up of records.

FINANCIAL REQUIREMENTS [STANDARDS 30 & 31 APPLY ONLY TO VOLUNTARY ADOPTION AGENCIES]
Outcome: The voluntary agency is non-profit making and is financially viable.

Standard 30: Financial viability

The agency ensures it is financially viable at all times and has sufficient financial resources to fulfil its obligations.

Procedures exist to deal with a financial crisis, including giving information to purchasers and liaising with them to safeguard the welfare of children.

Standard 31: Financial processes

The financial processes/systems are properly operated and maintained in accordance with accounting standards and practice.

The agency has documented financial arrangements for control and supervision of its financial affairs.

The agency has principles and standards, communicated to its managers and accountants:

- governing financial management, and

- describing financial procedures and responsibilities to be followed by the manager, staff, consultants, professional experts, directors and trustees.

The agency's accounts are maintained and properly audited.

The agency's trustees or management committee receive regular written information on the agency's finances.

SAFEGUARDING AND PROMOTING WELFARE
Outcome: The agency safeguards and promotes the physical, mental and emotional welfare of its service users affected by adoption.

Standard 32: Safeguarding and promoting welfare

The agency's service users are safeguarded from all forms of abuse, exploitation and discrimination, whether deliberate or inadvertent, in accordance with written policies and procedures.

For agencies providing support services to children:

- there is a written child protection policy;
- the policy and procedures cover what to do about suspicion or evidence of abuse/neglect and are consistent with the LSCB procedures and statutory guidance;
- staff and volunteers are trained in child protection and are aware of and have access to the child protection policy.

Allegations or incidents of abuse are promptly followed up and fully recorded on the service user's record and in a separate file.

There is a procedure for historical abuse allegations which may arise during service provision.

USER-FOCUSED SERVICES

Outcome: People affected by adoption receive appropriate, needs-led services and are treated fairly, openly and with respect.

Standard 33: User-focused services

People affected by adoption receive appropriate services tailored to their needs. They receive clear information about the service they can expect and its aims.

The agency's policies and procedures reflect the following:

- welcoming prospective users without prejudice and giving clear information;

- (for voluntary agencies) referring on if unable to meet user needs;

- listening to users' wishes and feelings, and considering their welfare and safety;

- listening to the wishes and feelings of children and giving their welfare and safety paramount consideration;

- (in England) considering the welfare and safety of adopted adults and their birth relatives when working with both;

- (in Wales) giving precedence to the wishes, feelings, welfare and safety of the adopted adult over their birth relatives.

The agency's systems can respond promptly to and work with people affected by adoption and always respect their race, religion, culture, language, sexuality, gender, disability and experience and understanding of adoption.

There are policies and procedures for working with people affected by impairments or communication difficulties or whose first language is not English (or Welsh).

The agency consults service users and seeks feedback, in appropriate ways for children, and records the results individually.

Effective three-way partnerships are developed where services are commissioned by an adoption agency and are regularly reviewed.

The agency tells service users how to complain or make representations and helps them do so if required.

SERVICE DELIVERY
Outcome: Service users receive a good-quality, professional service based on a needs assessment.

Standard 34: Service delivery

The agency has written policies and procedures for all its services and provision reflects the policies and procedures.

The manager knows what services are being provided and by which staff.

Prospective service users are told that they can approach the local authority for an adoption support needs assessment.

There is a written policy and procedure for deciding on provision of support services to particular users, and the agency takes account of any local authority adoption support needs assessment in making a decision.

Decisions to provide a support service are based on an assessment of the person's need for that service.

The manager ensures that staff providing services:

- clearly explain the service and obtain informed consent where appropriate;

- monitor and review service provision in each case, including how long to provide it and if it is meeting its aims.

National Minimum Standards Adoption Support Agencies*

Statement of purpose
Outcome: There is a clear written statement of the aims and objectives of the adoption support agency and the agency ensures that it meets those aims and objectives.

Standard 1: Statement of purpose

There is a clear written statement of the aims and objectives of the adoption support agency which describes accurately what facilities and services it provides and to whom.

The registered provider or the registered manager formally approves the Statement of purpose and reviews, updates and modifies it where necessary, at least annually.

The Statement of purpose contains the information listed in Schedule 1 to the Adoption Support Agencies (England) and Adoption Agencies (Miscellaneous Amendments) Regulations 2005.

An adoption support agency providing services to children produces a children's guide to the agency and its services and the guide is suitable for all children who come into contact with the adoption support agency. The guide primarily includes a summary of what the service sets out to do for children and is given to all children and/or their representatives. If necessary, the children's guide is produced in different formats to meet the needs of different groups of children to whom the agency may offer a service. The children's guide also contains information on how a child can make a complaint, including how to secure access to an independent advocate and how to contact the Children's Rights Director as appropriate.

Oral and written communications are available, when necessary, in a format which is appropriate to the physical, sensory and learning impairments,

* These apply to England

communication difficulties and language of the adoption support agency's users, staff and volunteers. Arrangements are made for those who are unable to understand the document to have it read, translated or explained to them.

The adoption support agency's policies, procedures and any written guidance to staff and volunteers accurately reflect the Statement of purpose.

All those working in the adoption support agency are aware of the contents of the Statement of purpose and a copy is readily available.

[The Adoption Support Agencies (England) and Adoption Agencies (Miscellaneous Amendments) Regulations 2005: regulation 5 – Statement of purpose and children's guide, regulation 6 – Review of statement of purpose and children's guide]

SAFEGUARDING AND PROMOTING WELFARE
Outcome: The adoption support agency safeguards and promotes the physical, mental and emotional welfare of people affected by adoption who wish to use its services.

Standard 2: Safeguarding and promoting welfare

The adoption support agency's service users are safeguarded from any form of abuse, exploitation and discrimination including physical, financial, psychological and sexual, through deliberate intent, negligence or ignorance in accordance with the agency's written policies and procedures.

Where the adoption support agency provides services to children:

• there is a detailed written child protection policy, including the management of and reporting plan for child protection issues;

• there are procedures for responding to suspicion or evidence of abuse and neglect which are in line with local Area Child Protection Committee

(ACPC) procedures to ensure the safety and protection of service users – this includes the involvement of the local authority and police and passing on concerns to the regulatory authority (where appropriate);

- the policy and procedures are in line with local ACPC procedures, *Working Together to Safeguard Children* and *What to do if you're worried a child is being abused*;

- all staff and volunteers are trained in child protection and are aware of the agency's child protection policy;

- all staff, volunteers and service users have access to the agency's child protection policy.

All allegations and incidents of abuse in relation to the agency's staff or volunteers are followed up promptly and the details and action taken are recorded on a file, kept especially for the purpose, and on the service user's record.

The adoption support agency has written procedures for dealing with allegations of historical abuse which may be made by service users during the course of service provision.

[The Adoption Support Agencies (England) and Adoption Agencies (Miscellaneous Amendments) Regulations 2005: regulation 12 – Arrangements for the protection of children]

USER-FOCUSED SERVICES
Outcome: People affected by adoption receive a service from the adoption support agency that is appropriate and tailored to their particular need. They are treated fairly, openly and with respect throughout their contact with the agency.

Standard 3: User-focused services

People affected by adoption receive a service that is appropriate and tailored to their particular need. They are given clear information about the service they can expect to receive and what the service is designed to achieve.

The adoption support agency has in place written policies and procedures that reflect the following principles:

- prospective service users are welcomed without prejudice and are given clear information on the services provided by the agency;

- where the agency does not provide the specific service requested, or is not able to meet the prospective service user's particular need, the agency refers that person to an appropriate agency or service;

- in deciding whether to provide a service, or which service to provide, the agency listens to:

  - the service user's wishes and feelings and considers their welfare and safety;

- where the service provision involves a child, their wishes and feelings are listened to and their welfare and safety are the paramount considerations;

- where the service provision involves adopted adults and their birth relatives, the agency takes into consideration the welfare and safety of both parties.

The adoption support agency ensures that systems are in place to respond promptly to requests and to work with people who have been affected by adoption, at all times being respectful of their ethnic origin, religion, culture, language, sexuality, gender and any disability and their experience and understanding of adoption.

The agency has written policies and procedures in place for working with service users with physical, sensory and learning impairments, communication difficulties and for whom English is not the first language.

Service users are consulted on decisions made in relation to their service provision and have the opportunity to provide feedback to the agency during and after the course of the service provision. The agency makes every effort to seek the views of any children receiving a service in a manner that is appropriate to their level of understanding. Consultation with service users is recorded on their individual records.

Where services are commissioned by an adoption agency, a three-way working relationship is developed with the adoption agency and the adoption support agency working in partnership to most effectively meet the needs of the service user. Commissioning arrangements are underpinned by a written agreement and are reviewed at regular intervals.

The agency informs service users of their right to make representations and complaints and they are helped to do so if this is required.

[The Adoption Support Agencies (England) and Adoption Agencies (Miscellaneous Amendments) Regulations 2005: regulation 13 – Provision of services]

SERVICE DELIVERY
Outcome: The adoption support agency's service users receive a good quality, professional service, based on their needs identified by an assessment.

Standard 4: Service delivery

The agency has written policies and procedures for each service it provides and service provision accurately reflects those policies and procedures.

The manager is fully informed of the current level of service provision with regard to each service provided by the adoption support agency, and is aware which staff are involved in delivering each of the services.

The adoption support agency has a written policy and procedure on how it will decide whether to provide an adoption support service to particular service users.

Prospective service users are made aware that they may be entitled to request an assessment of their needs for adoption support services from their local authority in accordance with the Adoption and Children Act 2002 and associated regulations.

When deciding whether to provide a service to a particular person, the adoption support agency has regard to the outcome of any local authority assessment of the person's need for adoption support services which has been conducted.

The registered provider ensures that, where the adoption support agency decides to provide a service to a particular person, the decision is based on an assessment of the person's need for the adoption support service.

The manager ensures that the individual responsible for the delivery of adoption support services to each individual service user:

- provides each service user with a clear explanation of what is involved in particular service provision and obtains their informed consent, where appropriate, to the service provision;

- monitors and reviews the service provision to each service user for whom they are responsible. This includes the length of the service provision and whether the service is delivering the outcomes that it is intended to achieve.

[The Adoption Support Agencies (England) and Adoption Agencies (Miscellaneous Amendments) Regulations 2005: regulation 13 – Provision of services]

FITNESS TO PROVIDE OR MANAGE AN ADOPTION SUPPORT AGENCY
Outcome: The adoption support agency is provided and managed by those who are suitable and have the appropriate skills and experience to do so effectively and efficiently to provide the services specified in the statement of purpose.

Standard 5: Skills to provide or manage

The people who carry on and manage the adoption support agency:

- possess the appropriate knowledge and experience of adoption law and practice and, where the adoption support agency provides services to children, knowledge and experience of child care law and practice;

- have business and management skills to manage the work effectively and efficiently;

- have financial expertise to ensure that it is run on a sound financial basis and in a professional manner.

The registered manager (or registered provider, where the registered provider is an individual and there is no registered manager):

- has a professional qualification relevant to working in an adoption setting (or children's services where the agency provides services to children) which is either NVQ level 4 or DipSW or an equivalent professional social work qualification; or

- is a Member (MBACP) or Accredited Member (MBACP Accred) of the British Association of Counselling and Psychotherapy (BACP), or is chartered by/registered with the United Kingdom Council for Psychotherapy (UKCP), the British Psychological Society (BPS) or the United Kingdom Register for Counsellors and Psychotherapists (UKRCP) or is registered as an Arts, Drama or Music Therapist with the Health Professions Council for England and Wales (HPC); and

- by 30.12.07, has at least two years' experience of working in an adoption setting (or children's services where the agency provides services to children) which may include managing an adoption support agency, within the past five years.

The registered manager (or registered provider where the registered provider is an individual and there is no registered manager) obtains a qualification at NVQ level 4 in management or another qualification which at least matches the competencies required by level 4 by 30.12.08, or following that date, within three years of registration.

N.B. Where the registered provider is an individual and does not have staff or volunteers, he or she is not required to obtain this qualification.

Appointees to the post of registered manager (or registered provider where the registered provider is an individual and there is no registered manager) who have no such qualifications begin appropriate management training within six months of appointment.

The registered manager (or registered provider where the registered provider is an individual and there is no registered manager) exercises effective leadership of the staff (where appropriate) and operation, such that the adoption support agency is organised, managed and staffed in a manner that delivers the best possible service provision for the agency's service users.

Standard 6: Suitability to carry on or manage

Any persons carrying on or managing the adoption support agency are suitable people to run a voluntary organisation or business concerned with providing adoption support services, and safeguard and promote the welfare of the agency's services users.

For the references set out in Schedule 2 of the Adoption Support Agencies (England) and Adoption Agencies (Miscellaneous Amendments) Regulations 2005, telephone enquiries are made to follow up written references.

The registered manager has a satisfactory disclosure from the Criminal Records Bureau in accordance with the Police Act 1997 as appropriate.

CRB checks are renewed every three years.

Records are kept of checks and references that have been obtained and their outcome.

[The Adoption Support Agencies (England) and Adoption Agencies (Miscellaneous Amendments) Regulations 2005: regulation 7 – Fitness of registered provider, regulation 9 – Fitness of manager, regulation 10 – Registered person – general requirements]

MANAGEMENT OF THE ADOPTION SUPPORT AGENCY
Outcome: The adoption support agency safeguards and promotes the physical, mental and emotional welfare of people affected by adoption who wish to use its services.

Standard 7: Managing effectively and efficiently

THIS STANDARD IS NOT RELEVANT WHERE THE REGISTERED PROVIDER IS AN INDIVIDUAL WHO IS NOT REQUIRED TO APPOINT A REGISTERED MANAGER.

In this standard references to manager mean registered manager.

The adoption support agency is managed effectively and efficiently.

The manager ensures that the adoption support agency is run in accordance with its statement of purpose.

The manager has a clear written job description which sets out the duties, responsibilities and level of delegation of the manager in managing the adoption support agency. The job description also specifies the person to whom the manager is accountable and/or who is responsible for ensuring that the manager carries out their duties and responsibilities. The manager must be notified in writing of any change in the person to whom they are accountable.

The level of delegation and responsibility of the manager, and the lines of accountability, are clearly defined.

Clear arrangements are in place to identify the person in charge when the manager is absent.

If the registered provider is an individual, he or she is only required to appoint a manger if he or she is (a) not a fit person to manage the agency or (b) is not, or does not intend to be, in full-time day-to-day charge of the agency. See Regulation 9 – Fitness of manager.

There are clear roles for the manager, staff and volunteers (where appropriate) and well established lines of communication and accountability between the manager, staff and volunteers.

The registered provider informs the manager, staff and volunteers of their responsibility to declare any possible conflicts of interest.

Standard 8: Monitoring and controlling

There are clear written procedures for monitoring and controlling the activities of the adoption support agency and ensuring quality performance.

The adoption support agency has proper financial procedures and there is a reviewing procedure to keep them up to date.

Information is provided to purchasers of services and others with a legitimate interest.

This includes:

- charges for each of its services;

- itemised amounts paid for services.

The adoption support agency's trustees, board members or management committee members:

- satisfy themselves that the adoption support agency is effective and achieves good outcomes for its service users;

- receive written reports on the management and outcomes of the services of the adoption support agency every six months to be able to monitor progress;

- satisfy themselves that all conditions of registration imposed on the adoption support agency are met.

Where the adoption support agency is an individual, he or she:

- runs the adoption support agency effectively and achieves good outcomes for its service users;

- produces written reports on the management and outcomes of the services of the adoption support agency every six months to be able to monitor progress.

[The Adoption Support Agencies (England) and Adoption Agencies (Miscellaneous Amendments) Regulations 2005: regulation 7 – Fitness of registered provider, regulation 9 – Fitness of manager, regulation 10 – Registered person – general requirements.]

Standards 9–14 are not relevant where the registered provider is an individual and does not have staff or volunteers.

EMPLOYMENT AND MANAGEMENT OF STAFF AND VOLUNTEERS
Outcome: The staff and volunteers who work in the adoption support agency are suitable to work with the agency's service users and they are managed, trained and supported in such a way as to ensure the best possible outcomes for those service users. The number of staff and volunteers and their range of qualifications and experience are sufficient to achieve the purposes and functions of the adoption support agency.

Standard 9: Suitability to work with service users

Anyone working in or for the adoption support agency is suitable to work with the agency's service users, in particular, children and young people where the agency provides services to children.

There are clear written recruitment and selection procedures for appointing staff and volunteers which follow good practice in safeguarding service users, and in particular children, where the agency provides services to them. All personnel responsible for the recruitment and selection of staff and volunteers are trained in, understand and operate these procedures.

All staff and volunteers working in or for the adoption support agency are interviewed as part of the selection process and have written references checked to assess suitability before taking up their duties. Telephone enquiries are made to each referee to verify the written references.

All people working for the adoption support agency, including those who wish to work on a temporary, sessional or voluntary basis, have a satisfactory standard or enhanced disclosure, as appropriate, from the CRB in accordance with the Police Act 1997.

No person is allowed to begin work until written confirmation is received that the outcomes of all status, CRB and reference checks are satisfactory.

Records are kept of checks and references that have been obtained and their outcomes. CRB checks are renewed every three years.

CRB checks for current staff and volunteers which need to be updated because it is three years or more since the last check was carried out, remain effective for a further three months from the date the Adoption Support Agencies (England) and Adoption Agencies (Miscellaneous Amendments) Regulations 2005 came into force (30.12.05).

Standard 10: Organisation and management of staff

Staff (including temporary and sessional staff) and volunteers are organised and managed in a way which delivers an effective and efficient service.

The work of all staff and volunteers is managed and monitored by people who have appropriate skills and qualifications.

There is a clear management structure with clear lines of accountability.

The level of management delegation and responsibility are clearly defined and are appropriate for the skills, qualifications and experience of the relevant members of staff.

The adoption support agency has systems in place to determine, prioritise and monitor workloads and assign tasks to appropriate staff and volunteers.

Professional supervision and consultation are provided at least six times a year for professionally qualified staff by appropriately qualified and experienced persons.

Volunteers are supported through regular, scheduled supervision sessions with appropriate staff.

Staff are supported to undertake ongoing training and appropriate professional and skills development.

Volunteers are supported to undertake ongoing training which is relevant to their work in the adoption support agency.

The adoption support agency has an adequate level of clerical and administrative support, office equipment and infrastructure to enable staff to carry out their duties in an effective and efficient manner.

Administrative procedures are appropriate for dealing promptly and courteously with enquiries from service users.

All employees, sessional workers and consultants are provided with appropriate written contracts, job descriptions and conditions of service.

All staff understand the role of the adoption support agency and there is a clear understanding (if appropriate) about how the agency works with staff in other agencies such as local authorities, voluntary adoption agencies and other adoption support agencies to achieve positive outcomes for service users.

All staff and volunteers have a copy of:

- the Statement of purpose;
- the child protection policy, where the agency provides services to children;
- the policies and working practices in respect of grievances and disciplinary matters;
- details of the services offered;
- the equal opportunities policy;
- health and safety procedures;
- the complaints procedure.

Standard 11: Sufficient staff with the right skills and experience

There is a sufficient number of suitably experienced and qualified staff to meet the needs of the adoption support agency and they are appropriately supported and assisted in providing a service.

The full-time equivalent staffing complement, in terms of numbers, grades, experience and qualifications, is sufficient at all times to meet the needs of the adoption support agency and is in line with the Statement of purpose.

Where a shortfall in staffing levels occurs, there are contingency plans to resolve them and to deal with priority work.

Staff policies encourage retention of salaried staff by providing support and training including flexible working conditions, training, regular supervision, study leave, clear workloads, terms and conditions.

QUALIFICATIONS

All social workers have a DipSW or equivalent professional social work qualification.

All counsellors, other than those providing birth records counselling under Schedule 2 of the Adoption and Children Act 2002, are Members (MBACP) or Accredited Members (MBACP Accred) of the British Association of Counselling and Psychotherapy (BACP), or are chartered by/registered with the United Kingdom Council for Psychotherapy (UKCP), the British Psychological Society (BPS) or the United Kingdom Register for Counsellors and Psychotherapists (UKRCP).

All Arts, Drama and Music therapists are registered with the Health Professions Council for England and Wales. Other staff involved in the provision of therapeutic services have appropriate professional qualifications.

Birth records counselling under Schedule 2 of the Adoption and Children Act 2002 is provided by qualified social workers who are trained and experienced in this type of counselling and who have a thorough understanding of the legislation surrounding access to birth records and the impact of reunion on all parties.

All medical advisers and other professional staff are professionally qualified and appropriately trained to work with those affected by adoption, in particular, the agency's service users.

All professionally qualified staff have appropriate knowledge and skills. This includes:

• an appropriate understanding of the Adoption and Children Act 2002 and associated regulations and guidance, relevant national policies and procedures, and where the agency provides services to children, the Children Act 1989 and its associated regulations and guidance;

• a sound understanding of the adoption process and adoption-related issues;

• capacity to work with the adoption support agency's service users;

• an appropriate understanding of the roles of other agencies who may be involved in the adoption process, in particular, adoption agencies, health and education services;

• an ability to promote equality, diversity and the rights of individuals and groups; and

• an understanding of the importance of the complaints procedure.

All professionally qualified staff keep up to date with current issues in the adoption field and developments in legislation and guidance.

OTHER STAFF AND VOLUNTEERS

Unqualified staff and volunteers carry out their functions under the direct supervision of qualified and experienced workers, who are accountable for their work.

Standard 12: Fair and competent employer

The adoption support agency is a fair and competent employer, with sound employment practices and good support for its staff and volunteers.

The adoption support agency has public liability and professional indemnity insurance for all staff and volunteers. The insurance policy covers costs arising as a result of child abuse claims against any staff and volunteers.

The agency has comprehensive written health and safety and equal opportunities policies for all staff, volunteers and service users which cover all legal requirements.

There is a written whistle blowing policy which is made known to all staff and volunteers.

Standard 13: Training

There is a good quality training programme to enhance individual skills and to keep staff and volunteers up to date with relevant professional, legal and practice developments.

There is a clear plan for ongoing training and appropriate professional and skills development of all staff and volunteers involved in the work of the adoption support agency, through induction, post qualifying and in-service training. All new staff are given induction training commencing within seven days of starting their employment and being completed within 10 weeks.

All volunteers undertake a period of induction which is completed according to a timescale agreed between the individual and the agency.

Induction training covers as a minimum:

- the aims, objectives and principles of the adoption support agency;

- health and safety policies and procedures;

- child protection policies and procedures;

- the complaints policy and procedures;

- policies and procedures for record keeping;

- the importance of confidentiality in the work of the adoption support agency.

There is an appraisal scheme which identifies the training and development needs of all staff and volunteers involved in the work of the adoption support agency. Individual programmes of training are available, outcomes are monitored and linked to assessment of staff and volunteer needs and relate to the tasks assigned to them.

All staff and volunteers are kept informed of any changes in any legislation, guidance and case law that are relevant to their jobs and are given the opportunity to attend regular staff meetings to discuss current practice.

The effectiveness of training programmes for staff and volunteers is routinely evaluated and reviewed and updated at least annually.

Training programmes reflect the policies, legal obligations and business needs of the adoption support agency.

Standard 14: Accountability and support

All staff and volunteers are properly accountable and supported.

All staff and volunteers have clear written details of duties and responsibilities expected of them, together with the policies and procedures of the organisation.

All staff and volunteers who come into contact with service users receive management supervision, and a record is kept by the line manager of the content of the supervision and of progress made. Supervision sessions are regular and planned in advance.

Staff and volunteers receive regular, planned appraisals from their line manager, which provide an opportunity to assess and comment upon performance and identify any training needs.

Each member of staff has the opportunity to attend regular staff and team meetings.

Volunteers have the opportunity to attend staff and team meetings where this is appropriate to their role.

[The Adoption Support Agencies (England) and Adoption Agencies (Miscellaneous Amendments) Regulations 2005: regulation 18 – Staffing of agency, regulation 19 – Fitness of workers, regulation 20 – Employment of staff, regulation 21 – Staff disciplinary procedure.]

INDIVIDUALS WHO ARE REGISTERED PROVIDERS

Standard 15 is relevant only where the registered provider is an individual (as opposed to a partnership or organisation) and he or she does not have staff or volunteers.

Outcome: The registered provider manages the agency effectively and efficiently and is suitable to work with the agency's service users. He or she is trained and supported in such a way as to ensure the best possible outcomes for service users.

Standard 15: Managing effectively and efficiently

The adoption support agency is managed effectively and efficiently and the registered provider is suitable to work with the adoption support agency's service users and to safeguard and promote their welfare.

The registered provider ensures that the adoption support agency is run in accordance with its statement of purpose.

The registered provider ensures that he or she has professional supervision and consultation at least six times a year with appropriately qualified and experienced persons.

The registered provider undertakes ongoing training and appropriate professional and skills development.

The registered provider has appropriate knowledge and skills. This includes:

• an appropriate understanding of the Adoption and Children Act 2002 and associated regulations and guidance, relevant national policies and procedures, and where the agency provides services to children, the Children Act 1989 and its associated regulations and guidance;

• a sound understanding of the adoption process and adoption-related issues;

• a capacity to work with the adoption support agency's service users;

• an appropriate understanding of the roles of other agencies who may be involved in the adoption process, in particular, adoption agencies, health and education services;

• an ability to promote equality, diversity and the rights of individuals and groups;

• an understanding of the importance of the complaints procedure;

• a clear understanding (if appropriate) about how the agency works with other agencies such as local authorities, voluntary adoption agencies and other adoption support agencies to achieve positive outcomes for service users.

The registered provider keeps up to date with current issues in the adoption field and developments in legislation and guidance.

The adoption support agency has an adequate level of office equipment and infrastructure to enable the agency to provide adoption support services in an effective and efficient manner.

Administrative procedures are appropriate for dealing promptly and courteously with enquiries from service users.

The registered provider has a comprehensive written health and safety policy and equal opportunities policy for all service users which covers all legal requirements.

The adoption support agency has public liability and professional indemnity insurance which covers costs arising as a result of child abuse claims.

All medical advisors are professionally qualified and appropriately trained to work with those affected by adoption, in particular, the agency's service users.

If the registered provider provides birth records counselling under Schedule 2 of the Adoption and Children Act 2002, he or she is a qualified social worker who is trained and experienced in this type of counselling and who has a thorough understanding of the legislation surrounding access to birth records and the impact of reunion on all parties.

[The Adoption Support Agencies (England) and Adoption Agencies (Miscellaneous Amendments) Regulations 2005: regulation 7 – Fitness of registered provider, regulation 10 – Registered person – general requirements]

COMPLAINTS AND REPRESENTATIONS

Outcome: Complaints and representations are resolved quickly and handled in a sensitive, thorough and non-biased manner.

Standard 16: Complaints and representations

The adoption support agency has a written complaints policy and procedure covering complaints and representations by service users, staff and volunteers. Where the agency provides services to children, procedures are in place to help them make a complaint if required.

The adoption support agency provides all staff and volunteers, others involved with the adoption support agency, service users and those who have been refused a service, with a copy of the agency's written complaints policy and procedure.

Any complaint is addressed seriously and without delay in accordance with the adoption support agency's complaints policy.

The complaints procedure:

• includes information on how to make a complaint;

• does not restrict the issues that may be complained about in relation to the services or the conduct of the agency;

• specifies how complaints will be handled;

• provides information on all other avenues for complaint where appropriate;

• is accessible to people with physical, sensory and learning impairments and those whose first language is not English.

All staff receive training in the complaints procedures covering the following areas:

• what constitutes a complaint;

- the procedure for dealing with a complaint and how this is recorded;

- to whom a complaint may be made outside the adoption support agency;

- the procedure to be followed should a complaint not be resolved promptly by informal means, including who should be notified and the keeping of records; and

- how a child can be assisted in making a complaint (if appropriate).

The adoption support agency maintains a complete record of all complaints made and how they are dealt with including the outcome.

The adoption support agency reviews the records at least annually to check satisfactory operation of the complaints procedure, to identify any patterns of complaint and action taken on individual complaints.

The adoption support agency takes appropriate action from any review in relation to its policies and practices, as well as taking any necessary further action in relation to individual cases.

A written record is made of action taken.

[The Adoption Support Agencies (England) and Adoption Agencies (Miscellaneous Amendments) Regulations 2005: regulation 16 – Complaints, regulation 17 – Complaints – further requirements]

Standard 17: Records with respect to services

The adoption support agency ensures that an up-to-date, comprehensive and accurate case record is maintained for each service user, which provides full details of that user's contact with the agency.

There are written policies and procedures on case recording which:

- are in accordance with regulation 14 of the Adoption Support Agencies

(England) and Adoption Agencies (Miscellaneous Amendments) Regulations 2005;

- establish the purpose and format of records;

- cover arrangements for maintaining the confidentiality of information relating to adoptions;

- ensure that manual/computerised indexes and case records are securely stored to minimise the risk from fire or water or other disaster.

All staff, including temporary and sessional workers and volunteers, understand the instructions and compliance is monitored.

Any decisions made in respect of a service user and the reasons for the decisions are recorded on case records and are legible, clearly expressed, signed and dated.

RECORDS
Outcome: All appropriate records are securely maintained, retained and are accessible when required.

Standard 18: Adoption case records

This standard only applies to adoption support agencies which were formerly Voluntary Adoption Agencies (VAAs).

The adoption support agency has written policy and procedural instructions in respect of the adoption case records of its predecessor VAA to:

- cover arrangements for maintaining the confidentiality of adoption information and the adoption case records and their indexes; and

- ensure that manual/computerised indexes and adoption case records are securely stored to minimise the risk of damage from fire or water.

Staff and volunteers understand the instructions and compliance is monitored.

Standard 19: Access to adoption case records

This standard only applies to adoption support agencies which retain the adoption case records of their predecessor Voluntary Adoption Agency.

In respect of the adoption case records of its predecessor VAA, the adoption support agency has written procedural and policy instructions which take into account the Data Protection Act 1998, the Human Rights Act 1998 and the Freedom of Information Act 2000 and cover:

- arrangements for authorising access to the adoption case records and their indexes; and

- arrangements for authorising the disclosure of adoption information;

- the circumstances where it might wish to make records or information available under the Adoption Information and Intermediary Services (Pre-Commencement) Regulations 2005, both within and outside the agency, for the purposes of its functions as an adoption support agency;

- how staff should deal with requests for such access or disclosure and who is empowered to authorise them;

- the requirement that, before the adoption support agency may make case records or information available, a written agreement must be obtained from the person to whom the agency wishes to disclose the case records or information that they will keep them confidential. This requirement does not cover the child or adopter but does cover anyone else within or outside the adoption support agency, including the agency's staff and volunteers.

Standard 20: Administrative records

There is a written policy on case recording, which establishes the purpose, format, confidentiality and contents of records, including secure storage and access to case files in line with regulations.

Separate records are kept for:

- staff, employed and independent/sessional workers and volunteers;

- complaints;

- allegations.

There is a system to monitor the quality and accuracy of records and remedial action is taken where necessary.

Confidential records are stored securely at all times and there is a clear written policy on access.

Written entries in records are legible, clearly expressed, non-stigmatising, distinguish between fact, opinion and third party information and are signed and dated.

There is a system for keeping records of all complaints made and for handling these confidentially and securely. Records of complaints and allegations are clearly recorded on the relevant files for staff, volunteers and service users – including details of the investigation, conclusion reached and action taken. Separate records are also kept which bring together data on allegations and complaints.

Arrangements are made for any records which are taken away from the adoption support agency's premises to be stored securely.

Standard 21: Personnel files for members of staff and volunteers

Up-to-date, comprehensive personnel files are maintained for each member of staff and volunteer.

Records are kept of the matters listed in Schedule 3 to the Adoption Support Agencies (England) and Adoption Agencies (Miscellaneous Amendments) Regulations 2005 on each member of staff and volunteer.

[The Adoption Support Agencies (England) and Adoption Agencies

(Miscellaneous Amendments) Regulations 2005: regulation 14 – Records with respect to services, regulation 15 – Adoption case records (adoption support agencies that were formerly adoption agencies), regulation 22 – Records with respect to staff, regulation 12 – Arrangements for the protection of children, regulation 17 – Complaints – further requirements]

FITNESS OF PREMISES

Outcome: The premises used by the adoption support agency are suitable for the purpose of providing the services as set out in the agency's Statement of purpose.

Standard 22: Fitness of premises

There are identifiable, suitable premises to which staff and others with a legitimate interest have access during normal working hours.

There are efficient and robust administrative systems, including IT and communication systems. Premises have:

- facilities for the secure retention of records;

- appropriate measures to safeguard IT systems; and

- an appropriate security system.

The premises and its contents are adequately insured (or there are alternative prompt methods of replacing lost items).

The adoption support agency has a Disaster Recovery Plan which will include both provision of premises and safeguarding/back-up of records.

[The Adoption Support Agencies (England) and Adoption Agencies (Miscellaneous Amendments) Regulations 2005: regulation 23 – Fitness of premises]

FINANCIAL REQUIREMENTS
Outcome: The adoption support agency is financially viable.

Standard 23: Financial viability

The adoption support agency is carried on in such a manner as is likely to ensure that it will be financially viable and have sufficient financial resources to fulfil its obligations.

Procedures exist to deal with situations of financial crisis, such as informing service users and those on behalf of whom the agency is providing services. This includes liaising with purchasers of services to safeguard the welfare of those receiving services and transferring case records where appropriate.

Standard 24: Financial processes

The financial processes/systems of the adoption support agency are properly operated and maintained in accordance with sound and appropriate accounting standards and practice.

The adoption support agency has clearly documented financial arrangements for control and supervision of its financial affairs and powers.

The adoption support agency has a clearly written set of principles and standards:

- governing its financial management, and describing the financial procedures and responsibilities to be followed by the manager, staff, consultants, professional experts, volunteers, directors and trustees, which are communicated to its managers and accountants.

The adoption support agency's accounts are maintained and properly audited.

The registered provider regularly receives information on the financial state of the agency.

The agency publishes its charges for each of its services and has a clear policy for the charging of fees and expenses for any additional services it is asked to provide. The statement is available on request to purchasers and others with a legitimate interest.

[The Adoption Support Agencies (England) and Adoption Agencies (Miscellaneous Amendments) Regulations 2005: regulation 25 – Financial position]

Part IV

Rules

Court rules

- The following part provides a summary of some of the key rules governing court procedure under the Act.

The Family Procedure (Adoption) Rules 2005

- These Rules apply to proceedings in the High Court, County and Magistrates' courts in England and Wales.

- Rule 4 requires active management of cases, including fixing a timetable and giving directions, encouraging parties to resolve disputes and dealing with different aspects of the case at the same time.

- Rules 20 and 21 allow courts to protect the identity of an applicant by means of a serial number and of any party by withholding identifying information.

- Rule 23 contains tables setting out the parties and respondents in the different proceedings.

- Rule 25 requires the first directions hearing to be within four weeks of the application and rule 26 covers what will happen at that hearing, including fixing a timetable for the case.

- Rules 31 and 32 provide for the final hearing including those who must be notified and who may attend.

- Rules 59–76 cover the appointment and duties of children's guardians, reporting officers and children and family reporters. Rule 75 sets out circumstances which would result in disqualification from appointment.

- Rule 77 covers disclosure of confidential reports to parties, including withholding a report in its entirety or deleting identifying information.

- Rule 84 sets out the documents an adopted adult has the right to receive from the court which made the order.

- Under rule 85, it will normally be the responsibility of applicants in Convention adoption proceedings to arrange translation of documents.

- Rule 108 permits agencies intending to place a child for adoption to seek directions from the High Court on whether to notify a father without parental responsibility (provided proceedings have not started).

- Rule 109 requires applications for annulment of an overseas or Convention adoption to be made within two years of the order.

- Rule 116 covers the application to adoption proceedings of the Human Rights Act 1998.

- Rules 154–167 deal with the appointment and responsibilities of expert witnesses, including their overriding duty to the court and the court's power to require joint appointment of a single expert.

The Rules are accompanied by practice directions which include the format for local authority reports to the court in applications for adoption/section 84 orders (Annex A) and placement orders (Annex B).

Appendix: Source material

Primary legislation

- Adoption and Children Act 2002

- Children Act 1989

Subordinate legislation

- The Adoption Agencies Regulations 2005 (SI 2005 No 389)

- The Adoption Support Services Regulations 2005 (SI 2005 No 691)

- The Independent Review of Determinations (Adoption) Regulations 2005 (SI 2005 No 3332)

- The Adoptions with a Foreign Element Regulations 2005 (SI 2005 No 392)

- The Adopted Children and Adoption Contact Registers Regulations 2005 (SI 2005 No 924)

- The Adoption Information and Intermediary Services (Pre-Commencement Adoptions) Regulations 2005 (SI 2005 No 890)

- The Disclosure of Adoption Information (Post-Commencement Adoptions) Regulations 2005 (SI 2005 No 888)

- The Restriction on the Preparation of Adoption Reports Regulations 2005 (SI 2005 No 1711)

- The Suitability of Adopters Regulations 2005 (SI 2005 No 1712)

- The Adoption Support Agencies (England) and Adoption Agencies

(Miscellaneous Amendments) Regulations 2005 (SI 2005 No 2720)

- The Special Guardianship Regulations 2005 (SI 2005 No 1109)

- The Adoption and Children (Miscellaneous Amendments) Regulations 2005 (SI 2005 No 3482)

DfES statutory guidance

- Adoption Guidance: Adoption and Children Act 2002 Statutory Guidance

Rules

- The Family Procedure (Adoption) Rules 2005

National Minimum Standards

- Adoption Agencies National Minimum Standards

- Adoption Support Agencies National Minimum Standards (England)

Note: This subject index is limited to the topics most likely to be sought within the primary legislation in Part 1, and to a lesser extent within the regulations summarised in Part 2.

CAE Publications

Below is a list of titles on various pieces of legislation published by Children Act Enterprises.

- *Children Act 1989 in The Context of Human Rights Act 1998*
- *Children Act 2004*
- *Child Protection*
- *Residential Care of Children*
- *Fostering*
- *'How Old Do I Have To Be?' (a simple guide to the rights and responsibilities of 0–21 year olds)*
- *Domestic Violence (Part IV Family Law Act 1996 & Protection from Harassment Act 1997)*
- *Looking After Children: Good Parenting, Good Outcomes (DH LAC System)*
- *Crime and Disorder Act 1998*
- *Sexual Offences Act 2003*
- *Anti Social Behaviour*
- *Children Act 2004*

Available from: Children Act Enterprises Ltd,
103 Mayfield Road, South Croydon, Surrey CR2 0BH
tel: 020 8651 0554 fax: 020 8405 8483
email: childact@dial.pipex.com

www.caeuk.org

Discounts for orders of 50 or more of any one title

1 903585 11 2

.99

Devon's
Railways
of Yesteryear

Chips Barber

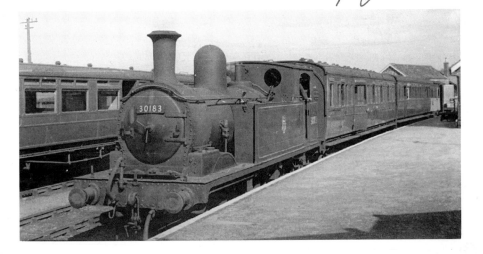

OBELISK PUBLICATIONS

ALSO BY THE AUTHOR

Railways On and Around Dartmoor
Place-Names in Devon • An A to Z of Devon Dialect
Around & About The Haldon Hills–Revisited • The Lost City of Exeter–Revisited
Diary of a Dartmoor Walker • Diary of a Devonshire Walker
The Great Little Dartmoor Book • The Great Little Exeter Book
The Great Little Plymouth Book • The Great Little Totnes Book
The Great Little Chagford Book • Topsham Past & Present
Sidmouth Past & Present • Honiton Past & Present
Dark and Dastardly Dartmoor • Weird and Wonderful Dartmoor
Ghastly and Ghostly Devon • Haunted Pubs in Devon
Ten Family Walks on Dartmoor • Six Short Pub Walks on Dartmoor
Beautiful Exeter • Colourful Dartmoor • Plymouth in Colour
Torbay in Colour • The South Hams in Colour

OTHER BOOKS IN THIS SERIES

Ashburton of Yesteryear, *John Germon & Pete Webb*
The Teign Valley of Yesteryear, Parts 1 and 2, *Chips Barber*
Brixham of Yesteryear, Parts 1, 2 and 3, *Chips Barber*
Pinhoe of Yesteryear, Parts 1 and 2, *Chips Barber*
Princetown of Yesteryear, Parts 1 and 2, *Chips Barber*
Kingsteignton of Yesteryear, *Richard Harris*
Heavitree of Yesteryear, *Chips Barber*
Kenton and Starcross of Yesteryear, *Eric Vaughan*
Ide of Yesteryear, *Mavis Piller*
Exmouth of Yesteryear, *Kevin Palmer*
Beesands and Hallsands of Yesteryear, *Cyril Courtney*
Beesands and Torcross of Yesteryear, *Cyril Courtney*
Sampford Peverell of Yesteryear, *Bridget Bernhardt & Jenny Holley*
Sidmouth of Yesteryear, *Chips Barber*
St Thomas of Yesteryear, Parts 1 and 2, *Mavis Piller*
Whipton of Yesteryear, *Chips Barber & Don Lashbrook*
Dawlish of Yesteryear, *Chips Barber*
*We have over 170 Devon-based titles; for a list of current books please send SAE to
2 Church Hill, Pinhoe, Exeter, EX4 9ER or telephone (01392) 468556*

Acknowledgements

I am most grateful to Mavis Piller for putting her large collection of old picture postcards at my disposal and to Ron Lumber whose excellent photography and advice has been much appreciated. Thanks also to Lens of Sutton. I would also like to thank the many people who have kindly loaned illustrations for this book. Finally, many thanks to Heather Somerwill for loaning the pictures which adorn the cover, taken by her late husband Alan. They are: front cover – Cowley Bridge; back cover – the incline between Exeter St David's and Exeter Central – Pinhoe Station.

*First published in 2001 by
Obelisk Publications, 2 Church Hill, Pinhoe, Exeter, Devon
Designed and Typeset by Sally Barber
Printed in Great Britain
by Colour C Ltd, Devon*

Devon's Railways
of Yesteryear

If you have read *Railways on and around Dartmoor*, you will know that I have a soft spot for the railways of the county, particularly the branch lines. This may be because, as the grandchild of a railwayman who chalked up 45 years of dutiful service, I was taken on many of the county's lines in the late 1950s and early 1960s. For many of the remoter railways this was to be the end of an era. Devon once had a considerable rail network but in such a small book as this, it is impossible to include but a fraction of the routes or scenes. The hope is that it gives a flavour of what some of Devon's Railways of Yesteryear were like.

The map below shows many projected routes whose proposed schemes never reached fruition.

Opposite, at the top, is a modest-looking Sampford Peverell Halt. It was a late addition to the main Exeter to Taunton line and closed in the 1950s. But later there was a need for a station here and Tiverton Parkway opened on 12 May 1986. Situated close to where the North Devon Link Road joins the M5, it enables those who live in North Devon to speedily access a rail route in and out of the region.

The middle picture opposite features the last train to stop at Exminster, between Exeter and Dawlish, on Saturday, 28 March 1964. Now those who live in this ever-growing village and work in nearby Exeter queue on congested roads into and out of the county town.

Opposite bottom, a train heads southwards through Starcross by the Exe estuary.

On this page, above, is Dawlish Warren in the early 1920s, whilst below is the view from Langstone Rock, a few hundred yards from the latter, looking along the coast towards Dawlish.

At the top of the opposite page is Dawlish, a popular destination for daytrippers from Exeter, many of them taking advantage of the 'sixpenny bathing trains'. The 'railmotor' was designed for local and light branchline work in the early 1900s. It was a locomotive and coach combined and driven from either end. Railmotors were gradually replaced by separate locomotives and coaches and all had disappeared by the mid-1930s. This photo is from 1909.

In the middle is Bridge House in Dawlish, which was, and still is, the railwaymen's convalescent home. The bottom picture shows a train heading out of one of the five tunnels between Dawlish and Teignmouth.

This is sometimes a most precarious stretch of railway line as the view above shows, with a train moving out of Teignmouth towards Dawlish. It is not unusual for this line to suffer storm damage. Beyond Teignmouth the line heads inland along the edge of the Teign estuary to reach Newton Abbot (below), once such an important railway town, which provided the livelihoods for many of the population. The photo dates back to about 1930. The station was rebuilt in the early 1930s. Today, in terms of the railways, it is only a shadow of its former self.

The main 'Great Western' line continues to head on inland and away from the South Devon coast. Having passed through the ancient town of Totnes, it skirts the southern edge of Dartmoor. Above is the former moorland-edge station named as Brent, meaning 'steep hill', in the village of South Brent. Below, about three miles further on towards Plymouth, is Bittaford Platform.

Opposite are three pictures of Ivybridge's previous station. The one which exists today was created to tie in with a park and ride scheme and is located beyond the viaduct, spanning the River Erme, seen in the middle distance of the top picture. When these pictures were taken Ivybridge's population was less than two thousand; now it is many times that. The large hill in the background is Western Beacon.

THE ERECTION OF THE
ALBERT
1857
SALTASH

Cornwood (opposite, top) was another village to have a station on this rail route but it was a tidy step to it for villagers. The middle scene is of Marsh Mills, a small station on the branch line between Plymouth and Tavistock South, which was sited a short distance north of the main line. Below that is a picture from 1857, just two years before the Royal Albert Bridge, spanning the Tamar, was completed. Brunel, who had engineered the route through South Devon, masterminded this precise construction with little room for error. In the past there were alternative ways of travelling between not only Plymouth and Tavistock but also Plymouth and Exeter. The 'Southern' line went around the northern edge of Dartmoor. Only parts of the line survive; the initial route northwards from Plymouth is now a branch line, which ultimately ends at Gunnislake on the Cornish bank of the Tamar.

Once the built-up parts of Plymouth, largely out of sight as the line passes through cuttings, are left behind, the beautiful Tamar Valley countryside is encountered; then, having crossed the Tavy, the lovely village of Bere Ferrers is reached. Above is its station. The line continues northwards to Bere Alston, today a railway cul-de-sac. Tavistock lies so near but so far. However, this is not a terminus as the branch line almost goes back on itself to cross the impressive Calstock Viaduct, over the Tamar. The line then climbs and curves its way steadily up to Gunnislake, passing through former mining country and giving impressive valley views along the way.

On this page we see Tavistock North, the station reached from Plymouth via Bere Alston after passing over a viaduct high above the town centre. Today it is possible to enjoy a leisurely walk across the viaduct. The station is now a house called Beeching's Folly. Evidence of this folly is visible in the appearance of the station following its closure (shown below). The line originally continued beyond Tavistock and along the western edge of Dartmoor.

The top two pictures opposite are of Brentor Station, whilst the one below is of Lydford, once an important junction where the 'other' railway, the branch line from Plymouth through Marsh Mills and Tavistock South, met its 'rival', on its way to Launceston.

The top picture opposite shows the viaduct at Meldon, between Lydford and Okehampton, whilst the middle one features the latter's station, this being half way up a hill and high above the town. Today the station has been beautifully restored and houses a visitor centre. Although the line from Okehampton on to Exeter is mainly a freight line, on summer Sundays, in recent years, passenger trains have been run between these two places.

Opposite bottom is a 1970s photo of North Tawton Station on this line.

On this page we have two stations on the former branch line which ran from Plymouth to Launceston, via Tavistock South and Lydford Junction. Above is Shaugh Halt whilst below is Clearbrook. The line through the Plym Valley, which opened on 22 June 1859, has largely been given over to use as a cycle track and makes a wonderful wooded ride. From Clearbrook back to Marsh Mills is downhill!

From Clearbrook the line passed under Roborough Down to Yelverton and then high over the Walkham to pass Whitchurch and reach Tavistock South, which is shown above.

Below is Mary Tavy and Blackdown, a few miles to the north-east of Tavistock.

Opposite are three pictures of the line beyond Lydford, the route, opened in 1865, having turned sharply westwards. Opposite top is Coryton, whilst below are two scenes at Lifton. The sign on the middle picture says 'Dried Milk Works' (I'm sure it does!). Beyond this the branch soon entered Cornwall at Launceston.

Opposite top is Yelverton. The station had an interesting lay-out, as trains passed through on the Plymouth to Tavistock South route but there was also a branch line leading up to Princetown. Perversely, despite an incredible rise in height, achieved by tortuous curves, these were 'down' trains. The first station encountered, before the Dartmoor hills took their toll, was Dousland, (opposite middle).

At the bottom, on a fine day, is Princetown, the highest point on the GWR. One of the 'passengers' seems to be looking for 'a sheep day excursion'! This line, which provided some memorable journeys, closed in 1956.

Above is Kingsbridge's former station, this being the terminus of a branch line, often referred to as the Primrose Line, which ran from South Brent southwards along the beautiful Avon valley. From here it passed through the hills to reach the market and head-of-the-estuary town by courtesy of Sorley Tunnel. The latter is now a tourist farm attraction and visitors can walk into the tunnel.

Below is the station at Gara Bridge, about half way along the Kingsbridge branch.

In the past there was also an alternative railway route for travelling between Exeter and Newton Abbot. The Teign Valley branch line left the main line just after passing through Exeter's St Thomas Station. It continued through the small Alphington Halt to reach Ide (opposite middle). Beyond this trains trundled through Perridge Woods and then a long tunnel to emerge at Longdown. After passing through another, shorter, tunnel the Teign Valley was reached at Dunsford Halt (opposite, bottom), this providing the natural southward corridor for the railway.

Above is Christow Station, now an attractively landscaped dwelling. With this line there seemed to be a pattern where the villages served by the route were a reasonable walk away. Christow, on the hillside, was a good example.

Below is Trusham, a stop in mining and quarrying country.

The next station (opposite top) along the line was Chudleigh, a bigger place than other settlements in this green and pleasant valley. However, there were times when it was also a wet one. The flood water from the adjacent River Teign occasionally reached a level to coincide with that of the platform. Beyond Chudleigh, what was the route of the railway is now the A38.

The picture in the middle is Bovey Lane Crossing, which was just beyond the small Chudleigh Knighton Halt. At this point the line ran through the generally flat Bovey Basin, geologically an ancient lake where clays, now heavily mined, were laid down over a long period.

Just beyond this the Teign Valley line reached its end by joining with the Moretonhampstead branch at Heathfield (opposite bottom). The bridge carries the A38 Exeter–Plymouth road.

Above, the scene of dereliction is the station at Bovey Tracey. The branch line which ran through here went from Newton Abbot up to the railhead at Moretonhampstead, a climb of several hundred feet.

Today, some of the track-bed is the Bovey By-Pass and some of it, northwards, above this, towards the lovely village of Lustleigh, can be walked for a mile or so. It's hard on the feet though! This village station (below), now a private dwelling, was used for a 1931 film version of *The Hound of the Baskervilles.*

Tiverton no longer has a station but this is how it looked. Like Chudleigh it occasionally was prone to flooding, the nearby River Lowman being the culprit. Rail travellers could travel either up and down the Exe Valley on the legendary 'Tivvy Bumper', now housed in the town's museum, or eastwards to Tiverton Junction to join the main line between Exeter and Taunton.

Below is a scene taken along this stretch of track. If you look closely you will be able to spot a continuous line of apple trees. This was the work of Joseph Diggle, a Lancashire fruiterer who often came to Devon to buy apples. On one of these visits he met and fell in love with a local girl and settled down in Halberton, close to the railway. He saw the potential for an extremely long and thin orchard and duly planted these Bramley trees, which he subsequently managed for many years.

Thorverton, about 8 miles from Exeter, was a station on the Exe Valley line. Above is the 'Tivvy Bumper' as seen at Thorverton. It is believed that this train has a ghost. In the early 1990s the owners of the former station, who had turned it into an attractive home, saw an apparition pass through one night – despite the fact that the space between the platforms had been landscaped.

The Bideford, Westward Ho! and Appledore Railway (abbreviated to BWH & AR) was part-opened, to Westward Ho! on 24 April 1901. But it was not until 1 May 1908 that the line was extended the short distance to Appledore making the entire, almost circuitous, journey from Bideford Quay to the port about 7½ miles, about twice the straight-line distance. In the summer and on a fine day it was a wonderful ride but when the elements were wild, as they can be in these parts, the journey was a tough one. In the teeth of a gale the engines struggled to proceed along the coastal section of the line. On 9 January 1904 Mr Chowins, the Bideford Borough Council Surveyor, issued a summons against the company because of the condition of the track along Bideford Quay, a lot of local people having fallen on the slippery lines. Its locomotives were commandeered for use in France during the First World War, the last engine leaving in July 1917 on a specially laid track across Bideford Bridge. None of them ever returned.

The Lynton and Barnstaple Railway was a narrow gauge railway that opened on 11 May 1898 and almost overnight made the stage-coaches between these two places redundant. However, those that plied between Lynton and Minehead kept going until 1920.

The Lynton and Barnstaple Railway was a superb line – it had to be to rise and fall so many hundreds of feet. Although the trains were slow the journey time was about half that taken by stage coach and, of course, a much smoother ride. The scenery and the views were stunning and as the line curved and twisted over Exmoor there were changing vistas almost all along the way. The locomotives which hauled the carriages on this $19\frac{1}{4}$-mile-long route were named after local rivers: Lyn, Lew, Taw, Exe and Yeo. Although the line was well patronised on Barnstaple market days, and during the summer, there was not enough custom to make it pay throughout the entire year. It is typical that in the April of its last year of operation, when a protest meeting to save it was held, most of those travelling to object to the rail's closure went by car! Its short life ended in September 1935 and the railway company were swift to dispense with it. Ever since there has been talk of the possibility of re-establishing it, even though it has now been gone for many more years than it was ever open.

Devon has a number of privately run railways. On this page the booking office and station at Buckfastleigh are shown. This line is the preserved South Devon Railway, which follows the Dart Valley and provides a lovely riverside ride to Totnes. It is possible to visit the town before making the return journey. On certain days, depending on tides, through tickets can be obtained from Buckfastleigh to Dartmouth. This includes the lovely river trip down the Dart. Another private line, the Paignton & Dartmouth Railway, runs from the former town down to Kingswear. Many take the opportunity to explore Dartmouth or to take the river trip up to Totnes and then the bus back to Paignton. The company operates such trips throughout the summer and they make an enjoyable day out. Sadly, the short branch line which left this at Churston no longer exists, but on the next page there are a couple of pictures of it.

Churston's station is located on a high point and the start of the two-mile branch to Brixham is seen to the right. The train was fondly known as 'The Whippet'. Shown above is number 1470, the last steam train to run on this line, which completed its journeys on 11 March 1961 and was replaced by a diesel locomotive. The line ceased operation in 1963.

Below is Brixham's station, which, despite the flat appearance of the 'scenery', was on top of a very steep hill high above the harbour.

Pinhoe is on the outskirts of Exeter and trains still pass through on the Waterloo line. Local trains stop but, apart from the former stationmaster's house, the station looks little like these pictures of yesteryear. It can be seen just to the left of the former station staff. The waiting room and booking office have been demolished, the footbridge has gone, and the signal box was carried away by lorry to be relocated adjacent to the railway station at Bere Ferrers in the Tamar Valley.

The only surviving branch line in East Devon is between Exeter and Exmouth. In the past there were others, as we can see here. Indeed, there was something of a network within this corner of the county and a perusal of the map on page 3 shows almost a railway rectangle. A line ran from Sidmouth Junction, now Feniton (opposite top) down the Otter Valley and through Ottery St Mary (opposite middle). Further south the line reached Tipton St John's, also known as Tipton St John (opposite bottom). Here it was possible to take the branch line to Sidmouth.

The picture above shows this line climbing steadily away to the left. Below, a locomotive heads along the Sidmouth branch and is seen climbing through a cutting near Harpford Woods. It is rumoured that Sidmouth's former station was sited well out of the town to deter daytrippers. A look at the way the lie of the land falls sharply towards the sea-front provides a more logical engineering reason for its location. The site has been developed for business use.

On the next page are three more stations found along the line which stayed with the Otter Valley. The pictures are presented in sequence. The one at the bottom is the station at Budleigh Salterton, whose site was later developed as a supermarket. Today much of the route between Budleigh Salterton and Exmouth has been turned into a cycle path, which makes a pleasant way of travelling between these resorts.